be not afraid

# be not afraid

FACING FEAR *with* FAITH

## SAMUEL WELLS

**Brazos Press**

*a division of Baker Publishing Group*
Grand Rapids, Michigan

Published by Brazos Press
a division of Baker Publishing Group
P.O. Box 6287, Grand Rapids, MI 49516-6287
www.brazospress.com

Printed in the United States of America

Library of Congress Cataloging-in-Publication Data

Wells, Samuel, 1965–
    Be not afraid : facing fear with faith / Samuel Wells.
       p.   cm.
    Includes bibliographical references and index.
    ISBN 978-1-58743-302-3 (pbk.)
    1. Christian life—Anglican authors. 2. Fear—Religious aspects—Christianity. I. Title.
BV4908.5.W438  2011
248.8′6—dc22                                              2011018135

11   12   13   14   15   16   17       7   6   5   4   3   2   1

For Charis

# Contents

Preface    ix
Acknowledgments    xi
Introduction    xiii

**Part 1    Be Not Afraid of Death**

1. How to Die    3
2. Does God Heal?    9
3. May They Find in You a Blessing    15
4. So Much for Servant Ministry    21
5. The Five Ws    27

**Part 2    Be Not Afraid of Weakness**

6. Is There a Balm in Gilead?    37
7. The Hound of Heaven    43
8. Speak Tenderly to Jerusalem    49
9. Many a True Word    55
10. I Have No Need of You    61

**Part 3    Be Not Afraid of Power**

11. By What Authority?    69
12. But It Shall Not Be So with You    76
13. Giving with Your Head, Your Hand,
    and Your Heart    83
14. Is There a Gospel for the Rich?    90
15. The Education of Desire    97

# Contents

**Part 4  Be Not Afraid of Difference**

16. You Are Not Your Own  105
17. Can We Talk?  112
18. Can We Still Call God "Father"?  118
19. Casualties of Destiny  125
20. The Three Realities of AIDS  131
21. He Is Our Peace  137

**Part 5  Be Not Afraid of Faith**

22. Time to Shed the Cloak  145
23. Born Again  151
24. What's Wrong with God  157
25. I Want to Know Christ  163
26. The Discipline of Joy  168

**Part 6  Be Not Afraid of Life**

27. One Day You Will Laugh  175
28. What Am I Going to Do with My Life?  181
29. Loving Yourself  188
30. A Criminal Waste  194
31. With Both Hands  200

# Preface

I have the wonderful privilege of being a pastor, writer, preacher, teacher, scholar, counselor, organizational leader, chaplain, university administrator, speaker, community leader, interfaith dialogue partner, mentor, and leader of worship all at the same time, and sometimes all on the same day. These reflections arise out of the intersection of these roles and opportunities.

But there is always something more important than what you are doing, and that is with whom you are doing it. And this is what has made the shaping of these reflections such a rewarding experience. Among those who have materially enriched the content of this volume are friends and colleagues, notably Jo Bailey Wells, Nancy Ferree-Clark, Abby Kocher, Meghan Feldmeyer, and Craig Kocher. Among the many who have in other ways shared the crafting of word and prayer are Rodney Wynkoop, Allan Friedmann, David Arcus, Gaston Warner, Keith Daniel, Emily Wilson-Hauger, Lucy Worth, Bob Parkins, Stanley Hauerwas, Ellen Davis, Kavin Rowe, Richard Hays, Greg Jones, Ray Barfield, Norman Wirzba, Tony Galanos, Richard Brodhead, John Kiess, Ana Kiess, Trygve Johnson, and David Hartley. Special thanks go to Rebekah Eklund, who has offered patience, humor, wisdom, and understanding in carefully and skillfully editing the manuscript and offering a great many modifications and improvements.

The book is dedicated to my sister, Charis Geoghegan. She appears in these pages, as she appears in my life, in sunshine and in rain, in joy and in tragedy, in timely counsel and in abiding companionship, in fear and in faith. I cannot imagine my life without hers.

# Acknowledgments

S ome of the material in this book has appeared in print before, in earlier versions, and I am grateful for permission to adapt and re-present it. Parts of the introduction appeared as "Intimacy and Fear," in *The Cry* 14, no. 4 (Winter 2008): 8–9. Copyright © 2008 by Word Made Flesh. Reprinted with permission. A version of "Casualties of Destiny" appeared in *Journal for Preachers* 32, no. 3 (Easter 2009): 17–20. A version of "With Both Hands" appeared in *Journal for Preachers* 32, no. 4 (Pentecost 2009): 3–5. A version of "Speak Tenderly to Jerusalem" appeared in *Journal for Preachers* 33, no. 1 (Advent 2009): 12–15. A version of "Is There a Gospel for the Rich?" appeared in *LiveSimply: A CAFOD Resource for Living* (edited by Annabel Shilson-Thomas, London: Canterbury Press Norwich, 2008). © Canterbury Press, an imprint of Hymns Ancient & Modern Ltd. Used by permission. A version of "How to Die" appeared in Stanley Hauerwas, Samuel Wells, and friends, *Living Out Loud: Conversations about Virtue, Ethics and Evangelicalism* (edited by Luke Bretherton and Russell Rook, Milton Keynes: Paternoster, 2010), 194–200.

# Introduction

This is a book of diverse reflections around a single theme. There may be some readers who sit and read it from cover to cover. But I suspect as many or more will visit different parts of the book as their appetite for encouragement in faith, challenge in discipleship, reassurance amid doubt, and exploration of the Scripture varies.

Each reflection is designed to speak to gut, head, heart, and hand—often in that order. Fear is a sensation of the gut. When I seek to assist others in meeting God in Christ, I begin with the gut. Whether writing, preaching, or offering pastoral counsel, the first questions I'm asking are: Where does this hurt? Why does this matter? What part of me can't rest until this issue is faced? What am I running away from? What can't be said? How can this paper, sermon, or conversation be the most important one I've ever written, offered, or had?

Although I have spent most of my working life in local churches, I currently work in a university context. And that gives me permission, indeed requires me, to speak to the head. And so the second set of questions I'm asking are: What is interesting about this subject? What is something I've never heard someone talk about before? How does this subject or part of the Bible connect to other subjects or other parts of the Bible? Is the Christian faith discredited in the face of suffering, science, and other faiths, or bankrupted in the face of imperialism, racism, and sexism? How can I bring faith to intellect and intellect to faith?

Once I have faced these first two sets of questions, the reflection has largely taken shape. Then it is time to address the third set of questions, those of the heart: How will these words move people? How will they be memorable—unforgettable perhaps? Rather than settle for conventional humility, how will these words become the most helpful or thrilling words their readers or hearers have ever read or heard? Why stop writing until I am confident they will be, at least for some? This isn't wholly or even largely about including stories or leaving room for humor. It's more importantly about realizing which are the points that really matter and staying with them while you give them a chance to take up residence in the reader's or listener's soul. It's also a question of balance. These reflections are designed to be read all at one go or one by one—but they are gathered together for a reason. If you write or speak always and only from and to the heart, you may be dismissed as sentimental or patronized as folksy. But if you are respected as someone who writes and speaks to and from the head and valued as someone who writes and speaks to and from the gut, then when you address the heart there is an element of surprise that means your words are more likely to have the desired effect.

The final set of questions concerns the hand. As a pastor and a theologian, my principal role is to explore and portray the wonders of God in Christ. It's often a mistake to be sidetracked too quickly by the question, "So what?" Such a question reinforces the reader's or listener's assumption that they are the center of the universe—which may be a big part of the problem. Nonetheless the reflections in this book are all written with a conviction that the Christian gospel shapes and reshapes every aspect of life, and it's important to point that out in appropriate detail with enough challenge to disturb but enough reassurance and encouragement to motivate. These questions are the simplest: How do I imagine my readers' or hearers' lives will be different after reading or hearing this? What do I want them actually to do? How do I feel about calling upon people to embody a lifestyle of which I am not an especially good example? Rather than constantly attacking bad examples of how people engage money, sex, and power, am I taking the time and the risk of trying to offer good examples in a realistic, thoughtful, detailed, and compassionate way?

Only when I believe I have addressed all four of these sets of questions am I confident that I genuinely have something to say.

The reflections in this volume are gathered around the theme of fear. I want to spend a few moments setting the tone for this book by describing how Jesus addresses fear. In doing so I am also seeking to illustrate how I go about speaking to gut, head, heart, and hand. Thus I hope to introduce both the form and the content of the book. I want to talk about fear, and about what the story of Jesus's transfiguration teaches us about fear.

I wonder whether you know what it's like to be terrified. I wonder if you've ever had that twisting screwdriver at the base of your stomach, that trembling shiver under your lower spine, that drying of the throat and tightening of the chest, the instinctive slow shaking of the head and the glazed staring of the eyes that says "Oh . . . my . . . God."

I want to take you into the mind's eye of Peter, James, and John after they followed the Jesus they thought they knew up a mountain (Matt. 17:1–8). They saw his face transfigured and become dazzling white, and they saw the Old Testament creak open and Moses and Elijah walk out of its pages, good as new, and park themselves on either side of Jesus. And then a big cloud came over like a flyover at the Super Bowl and the sky started speaking—that's right, the sky started speaking—about being Jesus's Father. And the three disciples did the obvious thing—they ran behind the sofa because they were terrified out of their tiny minds.

Fear isn't itself good or bad. It's an emotion that identifies what we love. The quickest way to discover what or whom someone loves is to find out what they are afraid of. We fear because we don't want to lose what we love. We fear intensely when we love intensely or when we think what or whom we love is in real danger. So a world without fear wouldn't be a good thing, because it wouldn't just be a world without danger—it would be a world without love.[1]

If you think back to times of intense fear, sometimes it's so horrible you can't bear to think about it. But sometimes it's different.

1. For extended reflections on fear that have shaped this and the next paragraph, see Scott Bader-Saye, *Following Jesus in a Culture of Fear* (Grand Rapids: Brazos, 2007). Bader-Saye offers an illuminating discussion of Thomas Aquinas's description of the object of fear as a future evil that is imminent, of great magnitude, and threatening the loss of something we rightly love.

Sometimes those fearful moments are periods when you feel most fully alive. I think that's because at those moments you're most aware of the things and the people you love. When you feel death or danger is near, you want to be with the people that matter in the places that matter, and you want to squeeze hands and hold people close and tell them what you need to tell them. After years of ignoring, forgetting, or neglecting those who mattered most, fear sometimes puts you right in touch with them. Sometimes you even feel a profound bond with complete strangers, based on common need or humanity. And maybe afterward you or they wish that a lot more of life could be like that.

We live in a time when politics is dominated by fear, and when politicians claim to be able to take away fear by somehow abolishing it. The phrase "War on Terror" suggests fear is something you can somehow kill. But our witness as Christians is to say that in some ways fear is a good thing, because it discloses our love. We show our faith precisely in the way we respond to fear, and in the way we show our love.

On the mountain, the disciples saw Jesus transfigured alongside Moses and Elijah, with the thundering voice from heaven declaring Jesus's unique identity and unlimited authority: "This is my beloved Son: listen to him." They were terrified. They thought they knew Jesus. They knew he was something special. He'd been voted MVP—Most Valuable Prophet—two seasons running. If it were today he'd have been on talk shows and T-shirts and YouTube by now. But this was something terrifying. Jesus was joined by the two biggest-name alumni in the Old Testament—and the whole of the history of Israel was present in him. Meanwhile Jesus was blessed and authorized by the voice of God, and clearly the whole presence and power of God was in him. He was the place where the closest humanity had ever come to God met the closest God had ever come to humanity. Not surprisingly, the disciples' legs turned to jelly. All the heightened awareness, all the hugging of strangers, all the screwdriver tummy and the shivering lower spine, all the realizing what they truly love and wanting to cling to what most matters—it's all here, because these disciples realize that *they're looking at the nature and destiny of humankind, straight in the face.*

Look at what happens next in the story. This is where we discover what Jesus does about fear. He does four things. "But Jesus came and touched them, saying, 'Get up and do not be afraid'" (Matt. 17:7). First, Jesus comes to the disciples. No shouting from afar, no ridiculing, no criticizing, no embarrassing, no trivial saying, "Hey, you guys, I guess you don't know my friends Mo and Eli—Moses this is Pete, Elijah this is Jamie . . ."—no, none of that. Jesus comes to them. He makes the first move. He makes the journey across their fear.

And then, second, it says Jesus touches them. Did you notice that? He *touched* them. I'll never forget the moment when I was told my mother was about to die. I was eighteen years old and three thousand miles away. Of course I was in pieces. A man I hardly knew started telling me mindless irrelevances about when his grandmother had died, but none of it mattered because what he did was to cup my hands in his and to look at me and hold me. He touched me. And I was not so afraid. And ever since then when I've trained people for ministry and discipleship I've said to them, "Maybe the most important thing in your ministry will not be what you say but the way you learn to hold people and to touch them when they are afraid." And so I look back at what Jesus does on the mountain and see that he touched each of the disciples before he said anything. He made the journey across their fear and he held them in the midst of their fear, by touching them.

Only then, third, does he speak. First he says, "Get up." Now this is interesting. The disciples are obviously still petrified. But Jesus has come to them and touched them. So now it's time for them to get up. Jesus encourages them to get up while they're still frightened. I wonder if these words mean anything to you. *Jesus invites them to get up while they're still frightened*. He knows they're still frightened. But, frightened or not, it's time to get up. The disciples have realized what they rightly love, but they are gradually realizing that what they rightly love is not genuinely threatened. It's just magnified beyond anything they could previously imagine and closer to them than they could ever have known. That's a lot to take in, but the best place to do it isn't face down on the ground.

Then, fourth and finally, Jesus says, "Don't be afraid." This hardly needs saying after the previous three things have taken place—Jesus comes to them, touches them, and raises them to their feet. They look up and they see what was there at the beginning of time and what will be there at the end of time: nothing but Jesus, nothing but

God's life so shaped as to be present to us. What they were afraid of turned out to be Jesus. And Jesus was there to touch them, raise them, and send them on their way.

Now we can see what has just taken place in this fourfold action of coming, touching, raising, and empowering. It's a microcosm of the whole gospel story. Jesus first *comes* to us in his incarnation. Jesus then *touches* us in his teaching and healing ministry. And then in his cross and resurrection and in the coming of his Spirit at Pentecost Jesus *raises us up* and *clothes us with power* and gives us reason not to be afraid. The whole gospel is in this single verse: and the verse begins with the disciples face down on the ground in terror. So if you feel like those disciples, feel like hiding behind the sofa because the truth is against you or putting your face down to the ground because reality is too much for you, then hear the gospel of Jesus Christ. Jesus comes to you. Jesus touches and holds you. Jesus gently puts you back on your feet. And Jesus says to you, "Don't be afraid."

Every time we pray, this story can shape what we hope for and what we think we're doing. We always come before God with fear: fear that our lives and our troubles are so large and looming, and God won't be *enough* for us; or fear that our lives and our troubles are so trivial and foolish, and God will be too *much* for us. Like the disciples, our heads are down and our face is in our hands. And as we pray Jesus comes to us. He makes that long journey of incarnation *every single time* we lie face down in fear. And Jesus touches us. He comes in Scripture, in insight, in pictures, in words, in wisdom, in kindness, but most of all in tender, uncomplicated, human form. And then Jesus tells us it's time to finish praying and get up. And then there's only one thing stopping us from setting about his business. And he deals with that by saying, "Don't be afraid."

My prayer is that this book may offer such moments of encounter with the transfigured Christ for all who read it. The heart of the gospel speaks into the most numbing and terrifying moments and dimensions of our lives, with words of hope and joy amid fear and bewilderment. The chapters in this book proceed on the conviction that there is no aspect of human existence that faith need avoid and that is not ripe for transformation by the grace of the gospel. This book is designed for the layperson seeking a direct articulation of the faith in relation to pressing questions of the day. It should also be of use to pastors seeking confidence to address complex issues in the light of the gospel. It is not a book about fear, but an attempt to address the gospel and many issues of the day in faith and without fear. Death, weakness, power, difference, faith, and life represent a fair selection of the kinds of questions Christians are sometimes reluctant to face head-on. This book is offered as an encouragement to Christians to do so and to find blessings and abundant life in doing so.

# PART 1

# be not afraid of death

The most important quality in a companion is their commitment not to run away from you when you are facing the
terrifying prospect of death. If faith in God can address
the subject of death, then it can be set free to speak to every other
aspect of life.

Fear is a terrible, isolating, paralyzing, numbing, echoing thing.
The person who loves you doesn't change the subject, say it may
never happen, go and get you lots of candy to cheer you up, or sit
you in front of the TV and try to distract you. The person that loves
you looks you right in the face and says, "I'm sorry." Those words
say, "It's frightening, it's humiliating, it makes you feel powerless
and frustrated and sad, but it's not going to scare me away, I'm not
going to make a joke or change the subject. I'm going to look right
into the heart of it with you and we'll stare it down together."

Of course we're all going to die one day, and we become so adept at
ignoring or obscuring that unalterable reality that it's easy to become
impatient with someone who's facing up to their own mortality. A
voice in each of us says, "What's so special about *you*? What about
*me*!" So the person who can look you straight in the face as you
name the truth of your own mortality isn't just crossing a barrier of

intimacy, they're resisting a childlike insistence that all the attention should be on them. That's what it means to be a companion—being with someone as they face how bad things really are and not changing the subject or drawing attention back to yourself.

To speak of faith in the face of death means to name our worst fears and gently but purposefully bring them into conversation with our deepest convictions. That is what the following reflections seek to do.

# 1

# How to Die

Woody Allen reportedly once said, "I don't want to achieve immortality through my work. I want to achieve it through not dying." Not long ago I sat by the bedside of a man who felt just the same way. He knew he had only a few days left to live. "I want to do something for my wife and my children," he said, "and maybe for my friends as well. I can't think of anything I can give them now, stuck here in this bed." I said to him, "Have you ever thought that you're more than capable of giving them one of the most precious gifts anyone could give, a gift all the more precious because it's so rare?" "What gift might that be?" he said. I waited to see if he would look at his circumstances and guess for himself, but after some moments of silence, I said, "A good death."

What is a good death? A good death is a window into the glory of God. A good death is a revelation of Paul's conviction that nothing can separate us from the love of God in Christ Jesus our Lord (Rom. 8:38–39). The reality of modern medicine is that relatively few of us will be fully conscious, lucid, and full of parting wisdom up to the very moment of our deaths. As one person said, "On the plus side, death is one of the few things that can be done just as easily lying down." The various tubes and machines will more often than not keep us technically going for some period of time after our last conscious thought or word. So we need to start getting our plans in order now, ahead of time, if we intend to give our families, friends, and society the gift of a good death. Preparing us for a good death forces us to live a good life. The less you can do about the length of your life, the more you need to attend to its breadth and depth.

We probably all know people who are either so worried about the future or so angry, regretful, or otherwise burdened about the past that they seem to spend little or none of their lives in the present tense. The first thing to hope for as we approach the reality of death is to find or receive the grace to be *present*, to live in the present tense. Finding the ability to live in the present is very similar to what many people call being "at peace." To live in the present tense and be at peace in the face of death requires two things.

First, it requires us to believe that the past is taken care of. This is fundamentally a matter of coming to terms with our humanity. Few of us can honestly say our lives turned out as we had hoped or expected. It's easy, perhaps natural, to apportion blame for that. If grievances and resentments are heavy on our heart and the gift of forgiveness hasn't accompanied a long journey of healing, it can be easy to blame others for everything. But we can just as easily blame ourselves. For a great many people, the difficulty of accepting forgiveness is at least as much of an obstacle to a good death as the difficulty of offering forgiveness. Yet we can also blame life (or God, whichever we choose to call it) for the quirks of science, nature, the economy, or history that made our lives less than we would have liked them to be. In the words of one rueful commentator, "Life is full of misery, loneliness, and suffering—and it's all over much too soon." Whether mocked or praised by others, whether starting from great privilege and prospects or from lowly fortune and station, whether littered with accolades and achievements or with setbacks and shame, so many of us regard our lives as more or less a failure.

In all these ways looking back on the past is coming to terms with our humanity, with the humanity of those around us, and with the limitations and weaknesses of the human spirit. Life and death are both about coming to terms with these limitations, and for the person who has learned to live with others, with themselves, and with the contingency of circumstances, we have a word: we call that person *patient*.

I noted above that living in the present tense requires two things, and that the first one is to believe the past is taken care of. The second one, which might seem even more pressing in the face of death, is to believe the future is taken care of. If letting go of the past is fundamentally about coming to terms with our humanity, opening our lives whole-heartedly to the future is fundamentally about coming to terms with God's divinity. The future is unknown. For many people the unknown that lies beyond the threshold of death is simply the most terrifying thing in all human comprehension, precisely because it defies human comprehension. I'm going to attempt briefly to break that terror down into its constituent elements, to make it easier to talk about.

For some people the big fear beyond death is judgment. For most of Christian history this has been what Christianity was really all about—preparing you to face the finality of judgment, and its bifurcation between heaven and hell. It's amazing how this has become so much less of an issue to people in the last 150 years, and consequently how attention has focused so much more on the conditions and possibilities and desire for justice in this present life. Nonetheless, the fear of hell weighs heavy on many of us as we approach death. While we may not imagine perpetual fire or gnashing of teeth, it's not hard to imagine being alone forever, a very gloomy prospect. And if one adds to that the possibility of everlasting pain, it's too oppressive to think about.

Perhaps the biggest fear for the contemporary imagination, captivated as most of us are by the realization and fulfillment of the individual self, is that beyond death lies simply oblivion. It is rationally hard to square the myriad complexity and texture of human existence before death with total emptiness afterward. But when we witness the mundane biological process of death in animals and plants, there can seem little observational reason for arguing that humans will be significantly different. As Johnny Carson is rumored to have said, "For three days after death, hair and fingernails continue to grow—but phone calls taper off." We're left with just our bodies and the worms. All the restorative qualities of sleep suddenly go out the window, and we are faced with a sleep without end, a complete annihilation of the self—for many of us, a horrifying prospect.

In the face of this, St. Paul writes these stirring words, which conclude the eighth chapter of his Letter to the Romans: "For I am convinced that neither death, nor life, nor angels, nor rulers, nor things present, nor things to come, nor powers, nor height, nor depth, nor anything else in all creation, will be able to separate us from the love of God in Christ Jesus our Lord."

Paul is addressing precisely these overwhelming fears—the fear of judgment, or at least of being eternally alone or perpetually in pain, and the fear of oblivion, of one's consciousness being wiped out of the drama of existence. He is telling his readers, "Each one of you is precious in God's sight. You are not merely biological human products. You are known, loved, called, redeemed, chosen. And you will be glorified. A whole set of forces may be against you—hostile others, troubling and extreme circumstances, even yourself—but if God is on your side, none of these will overcome you; indeed, *you* will overcome *them*, with something to spare. No power, nothing in the past, nothing in the future, no biological necessity, no demise of human cells, no amount of pain, and no sense of isolation will separate you from the love of God in Christ Jesus."

So in the face of our fear of *judgment*, the good news is that God in Christ is *for* us. This is what we discover in Jesus's healing ministry in Galilee and what we see when Jesus takes the world's punishment on our behalf on Golgotha. And in the face of *oblivion* the good news is God in Christ is *with* us. This is what we realize is God's earthly purpose when Jesus comes among us as a baby at Christmas, and what we discover is God's eternal purpose when Jesus returns to us as our risen Lord at Easter. God is *for* us and God is *with* us. "If God is for us, who is against us?" writes Paul (Rom. 8:31). This is the essence of the good news of Christ.

To bring these claims back to our mundane and needy emotional experience, our biggest fears about those we love are that either they will come to hate us or they will forget about us. Paul is telling us that in our eternal relationship with God neither of these eventualities is possible. God *cannot* turn against us and God *cannot* forget about us. Because of Jesus we will remain perpetually at the forefront of God's heart and mind. This is the gospel. This is the good news about the future that enables us to see our lives through to a good death.

That doesn't mean we don't still have fears about judgment and oblivion. The point about the assurance of Paul's words is that they enable us to face the future *in spite of* our fears about judgment and oblivion. Faith doesn't obliterate fear, but it enables us to live without being paralyzed by fear and thus to take the practical steps that witness to our hope beyond death. For the person who is able to live in this assurance, for the person who is able to find the grace to go on in the face of fear, for the person who can open their life to the unknown realm beyond death, we have a word: we call that person *courageous*.

And that brings me back to the conversation I had at that hospital bedside. The gift of a good death, that last and most precious gift one can give one's family, friends, and society, is fundamentally a witness of *patience* and *courage*. Patience to accept one's powerlessness to change the past, and courage to open one's life to the overwhelming unknown of the future. Patience to live with one's humanity, and courage to face God's divinity. That is what it means to make a final offering of a good death.

That's why it's so hard to accept that the practice of euthanasia can ever constitute a good death. The irony is that the word *euthanasia* literally means "good death." It's an awful thing to watch a loved one face a slow and painful, perhaps agonizing, decline toward an inevitable but perhaps relatively distant death. Few of us would find words to criticize a loved one who looked to a technological escape from a situation of progressive and extreme physical distress and debilitation. But our compassion shouldn't blind us to the fact that there's a genuine difference between passively withholding treatment and active euthanasia.

Continuing treatment, if treatment is no more than delaying the moment of death, serves no purpose. As Arthur Hugh Clough put it, "Thou shalt not kill; but needst not strive / Officiously to keep alive."[1] But actively killing, which is what euthanasia entails, is another matter. Killing those we can't cure and those whose pain we can't ease is an outright rejection of the claims of Paul in Romans 8. Euthanasia is a denial that God is for us and that God is with us. Euthanasia assumes that patience and courage are too much to

---

1. From Arthur Hugh Clough's poem "The Latest Decalogue," *The Poems of Arthur Hugh Clough*, ed. F. L. Mulhauser, 2nd ed. (Oxford: Clarendon, 1974), 205. In its original setting, the words are sarcastic.

expect of anybody. Euthanasia is a statement that perpetual oblivion is better than temporary agony. The legacy bequeathed by the practice of euthanasia is a world that has turned life into a disposable commodity, sees memory as a burden and hope as a fantasy, assumes friendship is inadequate and that we each die alone, and thus has no particular use for patience or courage, the only virtues that can really give us a good death.

Imagine a society without patience and courage. A society without patience is one that values only what can be had straightaway, searches for technological solutions to every problem, denies the existence of issues that can't be quickly and forcibly resolved, and ends up describing as solutions anything that seems to make the problem go away, even if the solution is worse than the problem. A society without courage has nothing to offer in the face of fear except perpetual distraction through entertainment, stimulation, or fantasy. It's a society that has left truth and reality behind and headed off in search of something less demanding.

And so a genuinely good death is a gift not just to one's friends and family but also to society as a whole. A genuinely good death not only requires and inspires patience and courage on the part of the individual, but it also requires and inspires a matching patience and courage on the part of family, friends, and society, because it can be a fearful and paralyzing thing to watch a person you love decline, diminish, and quite possibly suffer. If the dying person cannot, for good reasons or bad, find the resources to exhibit patience and courage, their family and friends simply have to supply the shortfall. A genuinely good death is a witness from all parties and to all parties that patience and courage are possible, even in the face of profound sadness, even in the face of crippling fear, even in the face of trying and distressing circumstances. A genuinely good death proclaims that God is for us and God is with us and nothing can ever separate us from the love of God. A genuinely good death is a window into the glory of God, a promise that, in Christ, the future is always bigger than the past, a moment of truth that says what lies ahead is not a threat of obliteration but the gift of completion. God has given us the assurance of God's love and the promise of God's presence, whatever happens. Let us resolve to give God in return the most significant witness we can offer: the gift of a good death.

8

# 2

# Does God Heal?

As far as I can tell, there are two kinds of healing in the church. We could call them "Loud Healing" and "Quiet Healing." Loud Healing involves a lot of shouting, uses plenty of expansive hand gestures, and tends to be much featured on daytime television. Quiet Healing uses words like *wholeness* and *journey* a lot, tends to avoid large crowds, and is pretty resistant to definitions—except that it knows it wants to keep a mighty long way from Loud Healing.

Naaman the Syrian, the large-egoed general at the center of 2 Kings 5, is clearly in the Loud Healing camp. Second Kings describes Naaman as the "commander of the army of the king of Aram," a "great man," a "mighty warrior" who is "in high favor" with his master the king. Naaman has one problem: he suffers from leprosy, and when his wife's Israelite servant girl tells him he could find healing in the land of Israel, Naaman seizes the opportunity. He sets off for Israel in pomp and circumstance, with all his horses and chariots, and arrives at the prophet Elisha's house expecting a spectacular show. He wants a big audience, including the king of Israel, he's happy to write a fat check, and he wants Elisha to stand before him and wave his hands around and perform a spectacular cure. In the end, Naaman *is* healed, but it's not a Loud Healing that heals him. It's the quiet words of a servant girl and a simple washing in the River Jordan that end up making his skin as smooth as that of a young boy. He moves from arrogance to demand, from demand to disappointment, from disappointment to humility, and from humility to simple obedience. "If the prophet had commanded you to do something difficult," ask his servants, "would you not have done it? How much more, when all he said to you was, 'Wash, and be clean'?" (2 Kings 5:13). Turned out Naaman had to be healed of his pretension before he could be healed of his leprosy. No Loud Healing for him. By the end, God has not only given this man a fresh body, but God has also put a new man *in* that body.

There are a lot of healing stories in the Scriptures, and it's easy to glaze over and think, "That's just another healing story." It becomes one of the greatest barriers between ourselves and the world of the Bible: back then healings seemed to be two a penny, while today they seem very rare indeed. It gets us into the habit of thinking the Bible isn't really a story about us. But in fact there's no such thing as "just a healing story." Every healing story in the Bible is there for a reason and is telling us something specific about salvation, because in the Bible healing and salvation are more or less the same thing. We find that hard to grasp because we've got hold of the idea that healing is a present thing for the body while salvation is a future thing for the soul. But that's not what the New Testament is saying. For the Bible, salvation is a personal, social, and cosmic thing that refers to everything God wants for us and every way God touches our lives. Healing is the same.

One Friday night when I was a young teenager my mother sat me down on the sofa and said, "Samuel, I have something to tell you." Those words have ever since sent cold shivers down my spine. She held my hand and she said, "I'm going to die. The cancer in my body is not going to get better, and in a few months it's going to kill me." I was stunned. It turned out she was right. She didn't get better. And some while later, just as she said, she died. And from the moment she told me to the moment she died I never once prayed for her to be healed. Ours was a household that didn't do Loud Healing. My mother had been a nurse. For her it was about accepting facts.

10

And yet ever since, I've wondered whether my refusal to pray for healing was a lack of faith on my part—a desire to protect myself from disappointment, a resistance to showing God how naked and defenseless I was, an urge perhaps more than anything else to protect God from my own anger, despair, and terror. I'm not saying that if I'd prayed for healing my mother would have gotten better. I'm not saying that it's fair to judge a kid who is out of his depth in every way. But I am saying that if salvation is what the gospel is about, then healing is something we pray for, and that my reluctance to do so was more about self-protection and a misguided God-protection than it was about faith. The gospel and healing don't always come together, but they're wrapped up in one another. The mistake is to assume we can have one without the other.

To understand the relationship between healing and salvation we need to name precisely what salvation is. It's about the past and the future. Salvation is the transformation of our past from a burden to a gift, from a place of grief and regret to a heritage of wisdom and joy. And salvation is the transformation of our future from curse to a blessing, from a place of fear and death to a destiny of hope and glory. When we talk about the salvation of the past we call it *the forgiveness of sins*. When we talk about the salvation of the future we call it *eternal life*. These are the gifts Jesus brought in his life, death, and resurrection: the forgiveness of sins and eternal life. The restoration of the past and the promise of the future. This is what salvation is.

So what is healing? Well, we know that even when we've been forgiven, there's still a mess to clear up. Forgiveness takes away the guilt, blame, enmity, and shame, but it doesn't immediately take away the pain, loss, hurt, and damage. Something else is required. And we also know that eternal life may last forever, but there are some parts of it we'd like right now, because there are parts of ourselves, our lives, our relationships, and our communities that are diseased, deathly, disordered, and distressed. Something is required right now, a kind of advance payment of eternal life. And the name we give to those two things, the part that remains to be done when forgiveness has done its work and the part that we need to be done right now despite our hope for life eternal, is the same name: "healing." Healing is the third part of salvation, the part sandwiched between forgiveness and eternal life. Salvation means there's forgiveness, there's eternal life, and in between, filling up any space that may linger between forgiveness and everlasting life, there's healing.

Some while ago I was talking with a friend who teaches at a boarding school. He told me of a fourteen-year-old boy dying of cancer and how it was dominating the life of the whole school, testing everyone's faith to the limit. I decided to leave my compassionate pastoral hat on the peg for a few minutes and ask some simple, direct questions.

"Does the boy have any friends?"

"Oh yes," said my friend, "he's found who his true friends are and made some of the deepest friendships between teenage boys I've ever seen."

"How are the boy's parents?"

"It's wonderful how the whole community has embraced them like an extended family, and they often turn up during the week unannounced and stay over."

"Does the boy have faith?"

"You know, he wasn't one of the especially religious ones, but I've often been with him and given him the sacrament and kept silence and held his hand and there's an incredible feeling in that room."

"I guess this must have been your worst semester in teaching."

"Well, you know, in a way it's been my best, because there's been a meaning and purpose about the whole school I've never known before. It almost feels like a transfiguration."

And then I took a risk and said, "What you're describing doesn't sound like hell. It sounds like the kingdom of God. This boy isn't being healed, but he sure is bringing salvation."

There was a long silence. My friend was in tears. I wish now we'd hugged, but you have to understand we are male and British so instead we talked about England's soccer team and whether there was any chance the new coach would get them to the World Cup finals. My friend's head was spinning, and he needed a bit of time for his breaking heart to catch up. By the end of the walk his anger and bewilderment was turning to thankfulness and an extraordinary kind of joy.

These are things you only get to say to a very close friend or a complete stranger. What I was trying to explain was that if you've truly known the forgiveness of sins, and if eternal life really has intruded on your here and now, healing may not be quite so important to you, because healing names the gap between forgiveness and eternal life, and very occasionally, like at that school, the gap is actually very small. Of course they still longed for the boy to recover, but forgiveness had done its work, eternal life was very tangible, and the kingdom of God was close at hand. If you have forgiveness and eternal life, you don't need healing quite as badly. You don't have to believe that God sent the cancer or that suffering has a purpose or any of that stuff—you just have to see that God offers us forgiveness and eternal life, and sometimes in our most extreme situations we and those around us are more aware of that than ever.

Around fifteen years ago I had a young man in my adult confirmation class. He walked a bit on the wild side and his girlfriend was pretty wild too, although she didn't always walk on the same wild side that he walked on. One morning I heard from her that they'd split up and that she hadn't seen him in days. An hour later I heard he'd woken up twelve hours after taking a bottle of Tylenol. I sat with him in the hospital as he lost consciousness, his liver long gone. His brothers had turned up from all over the country, and their sober conclusion was that he was dying as impetuously and tragically as he'd lived, leaving a long trail of emotional and physical wreckage behind him. The following morning I got a call to say he'd been given a liver transplant and was regaining consciousness. I couldn't believe it. I rushed to the ward and to my dismay I found the angriest man I've ever seen. He'd meant to commit suicide, was discovering he'd been foiled, and was incandescent with rage.

I tell this story because by sheer medical criteria it ought to be a story of healing. But it obviously isn't. There's more to healing than getting a new liver when you've destroyed your old one. I tell the story because it's the opposite of the fourteen-year-old boy in the school. What my teacher friend discovered was that when you have forgiveness and eternal life, you don't need healing quite as badly. What my wild friend discovered was that if you're a million miles from forgiveness and eternal life, healing isn't really going to help you. At that boarding school, forgiveness and eternal life were so close that the kingdom of God had come very near. In that critical care ward, forgiveness and eternal life were so far away there was simply way too much for healing to do on its own.

13

What we *think* we need is healing. What we *truly* need is forgiveness and eternal life. Sometimes we get healing; sometimes we don't. If we get healing in the context of forgiveness in the past and the hope of eternal life in the future, it's a kind of fulfillment of forgiveness and an anticipation of eternal life. If we get healing in the absence of the things we really need, we may find it pretty much useless.

And that brings us back to Naaman. He comes down from Syria, pumping his chest and demanding healing. But Elisha is too "busy" to see him. Of course Elisha's not really sitting in his study taking a conference call from the state department. He's teaching Naaman a lesson. "If you receive healing right now," Elisha's saying, "that healing isn't going to help you." Naaman's got to get down from his high horse and chariot first. And at the end of the story Naaman praises and worships the God of Israel. Here's our context: forgiveness and eternal life—restored relationships and the dismantling of death in the face of God's glory. And sandwiched in between, healing. Healing is the only context in which it makes any sense.

"What can I get you, sir?" "I'll take a healing, please." "Would you like that with forgiveness and eternal life, sir?" "No thanks, I'll take it as it comes." That's the human condition. We want healing without salvation. But God offers us forgiveness of sins and life eternal. That's salvation. That's where healing is truly to be found. And sometimes sandwiched in between is healing—but sometimes not. And of course we long for the healing. Of course we do. I did as a kid; my friend did at his school; everyone has at some time or other, sometimes maybe even more deeply than anything they know. And of course we pray. And what God gives us over and over again is forgiveness and eternal life, everything we need in the past and everything we could imagine for the future. And sometimes they are so close together that we call it healing, and sometimes even when they aren't especially close together healing comes and fills that gap, and sometimes healing comes but forgiveness and eternal life are so far away that the healing is no good to us.

So the question, does God heal? can only be asked alongside the question, does God save? And these are the answers. Does God *heal* me? Sometimes. Does God *save* me? Always. Always. Always.

# 3

# May They Find
# in You a Blessing

Every two or three years I go away on my own for a morning
and write my own obituary. I've probably done it half a dozen
times now. The whole point is to look ahead a few years and
write the most glowing things I could ever wish someone to say
about me. I look at the mundane and unremarkable details of my
life to this point and see them as merely introductory material to
the glory that is to come. (I commended the exercise to a friend of
mine who's a monk. He struggled to take it seriously, and insisted
on saying, "Died peacefully in his bed, surrounded by two of his
favorite wives.") Writing it all down usually takes me about three
hours. When I've finished I look back at this marvelous person I've
described and wonder, "Why can't I live like that now? If that's
what I admire, why isn't that who I am? What's *stopping* me?" What
begins as an exercise in pride and vainglory ends as a humbling act
of confession and renewal.

I wonder what it would be like to write an obituary for Abraham.
It might begin a little bit like this. God had a plan. That plan was
to be in relationship: to be a friend, a sharer of joys and sorrows, a

15

faithful and persevering companion. And so there was creation—sun, moon, stars, and all the rest—and the crown of that creation was humanity, expressed as Adam and Eve. *Adam* means "earth" and *Eve* means "life." Humanity is the place where the life that comes from the heart of God most actively intersects with the earth that comes from the hand of God. This, then, was God's good intention: out of matter and spirit to make humanity, and in relation to humanity to express the heart of God. That was plan A.

But plan A was foiled. Sin entered the story. God's intention had a devastating setback. The human relationship with God became one of deceit and suspicion and fear—and, as the story of Cain killing his brother Abel shows, human relationships with one another became ones of distrust, envy, and violence. This distrust, envy, violence, deceit, suspicion, and fear became so overwhelming that God lost patience and decided to wipe the slate clean and begin all over again.

So there was a second plan, plan B. This time the plan wasn't to be in relationship with the whole of humanity from the beginning. This time the plan was to find one righteous person, and build from there. Plan B was called Noah. Noah was the one righteous man whose family God saved from the carnage of the flood. It's amazing that Noah's ark is the number one Bible story read to children because it's the most wholesale destruction of human beings and creation ever described. But plan B didn't work out either. Noah fouled it up within a couple of verses of getting off the ark.

Later, when people moved toward civilization in cities, the story of the Tower of Babel recounts the way people resisted God's gift of diversity by trying to force humanity into one grand scheme.

So the plan for a relationship with all humanity failed and the plan for a relationship through one righteous man failed, and God came up with a third plan. And this is where Abraham comes in. God's third plan was a relationship with one people, the family of Abraham. In a way, plan C is a combination of the previous two. It has the corporate dimension of the first plan and the holiness dimension of the second plan. Abraham's children are to be God's holy people, and through them God will come into relationship with all peoples once again. This is plan C, and plan C is what the Old Testament is all about.

That's how Abraham's obituary begins. But what would be a perfect ending for Abraham's obituary? Of course it would include a catalog of his achievements: the prize for best patriarch, the prize for the longest walk in the Bible, and no doubt the prize for the best beard in the Old Testament. But wouldn't it be amazing if there were to be a person who appeared and expressed a perfect relationship between God and humanity? Wouldn't it be amazing if a person came along who represented the new creation embodied in Adam and Eve, the holiness and righteousness represented in Noah, and the corporate dimension of the chosen people represented by Abraham? In other words a person who fulfilled plans A, B, and C?

That's what the Christian faith proclaims. God's plan for and promises to Adam and Noah are not invalidated by the promises to Abraham, but are fulfilled in the coming of Christ. Jesus is a Jew who validates all the previous plans of God. Jesus is all three plans restored. He is the new creation like Adam and Eve, he is the one righteous man like Noah, and he is the embodiment and inaugurator of the chosen people like Abraham.

Let's look a bit more closely at what God says to Abraham in the vital first three verses of Genesis 12. These three verses are so crucial we could call them the manifesto of the Old Testament. If you look carefully, you see God makes seven promises to Abraham. Number one, "I will make of you a great nation." Number two, "I will bless you." Number three, I will "make your name great." Number four, "You will be a blessing." Number five, "I will bless those who bless you." Number six, "The one who curses you I will curse." Number seven, "In you all the families of the earth shall be blessed."

Now there's a great deal in this sevenfold blessing that excites some people and equally dismays others. There are broadly two issues at stake.

The first is that since it follows the words "Go from your country and your kindred and your father's house to the land that I will show you" it seems like a title deed to the real estate called Canaan. Abraham's call and Abraham's blessing are about land and family, and, so the argument goes, to say today that these words aren't really about the land of Israel is as absurd as saying today that these words aren't about the Jews.

The second issue is the so-called prosperity gospel movement. When you switch on your TV you don't need to browse too many channels before you see a man in a sharp suit walking around a packed auditorium proclaiming that God wants to bless you, and that blessing means health and wealth, and that if you don't have health or wealth it's because you haven't asked for them, and what you need to do now, besides sending a donation to this number appearing on your screen, is to name that blessing and claim that blessing, just as God granted the request of Jabez who in 1 Chronicles called out and said, "Oh that you would bless me and enlarge my border, and that your hand might be with me, and that you would keep me from hurt and harm!" (4:10). It's not surprising that the prosperity gospel is popular for those in tough circumstances and is rapidly catching on in Africa, because a lot of people could use a whole lot more health and wealth.

But the theological claimants of the Zionist movement and the prosperity gospel need to look a little more closely at the sevenfold promise God makes to Abraham. The middle one of God's seven promises says, "You will be a blessing." Not you will *receive* a blessing, but you will *be* a blessing. And if Abraham didn't get it, or needed a little bit more help identifying what this interesting phrase might mean, it's repeated in more detail in God's seventh and climactic promise at the end: "*In you all the families of the earth shall be blessed.*" Here we discover what blessing is really all about. Blessing is not fundamentally about the security that comes through more land, children, spouses, camels, donkeys, SUVs, pages on your CV, university degrees, houses, holidays, awards, endowments, guns, clothes, or body enhancements. Blessing is fundamentally about others being able to trace their sense of well-being, peace, and joy to *you*. God is saying to Abraham, "I wanted all humankind to be a source of well-being, peace, and joy to one another and to me. But it didn't work out like that. So I thought I'd try to condense all that well-being, peace, and joy in one person. But that didn't work either. So I'm going to try to convey all the well-being, peace, and joy I have to give the world through one special people, and that people will be the people I give the world through you."

So the three questions we can ask ourselves about whether a blessing is true and one we should rightly seek derive from the three plans

18

of God set out in the first twelve chapters of Genesis. Question one: is this blessing fundamentally something everyone can have; is it based in our common humanity? (The Adam and Eve question.) Question two: is this blessing fundamentally about being holy, about being shaped and fitted to serve God in body, mind, and spirit? (The Noah question.) And question three: is this blessing one I am expecting to share with others, or is it something I'm expecting to keep to myself? (The Abraham question.)

Let's see how theological Zionism shapes up to these three questions. (Don't get me wrong—I'm not questioning the legitimacy of the State of Israel; I'm simply asking whether it's fair to describe the State of Israel as God's blessing in the light of Genesis 12, as a lot of people do.) One, is the State of Israel a place where all people can find blessing, or just a few? Two, is the State of Israel fundamentally about making a holy people? Three, is the State of Israel looking to share well-being, peace, and joy with others, or to keep them to itself? Those seem to be the questions. And as for the prosperity gospel: Are our prayers for health and wealth matched by prayers for the health and wealth of others across the whole spread of humanity? Are such prayers matched by a longing to be holy? Is that health and wealth something we are expecting to share with others, or is it something we're expecting to keep to ourselves? I'm not going to answer any of these questions. But I'm not going to hide the fact that some of them answer themselves.

The point of blessing—in Genesis, in Jesus, and today—is that we should become people through whom others find well-being, peace, and joy. God's most important promise to Abraham was, "Through you all the peoples of the earth will find a blessing." And before the church becomes too self-righteous about criticizing Zionism or the prosperity gospel, we need to ask ourselves the same questions. Is our gospel and church life something everyone can have? Is it making us holy? Is it fundamentally a shared thing, or something we see as primarily for us as individuals? If God has given the Holy Land to Israel, it is not to keep Israel safe but so that Israel may be a blessing for all the families of the earth. If God has given you prosperity, it's not to protect you from others, but so that your life, your home, and your resources may become ways in which others may find a blessing.

19

I want to take you back to that obituary I mentioned at the beginning. Yes, an obituary is full of events, achievements, births, marriages, and deaths. But if you're anything like me, you skip ahead past the ponderous narrative to the final paragraph, which says something like, "above all, she will be remembered for her . . ."—and then it describes what she was really like. And that's not about skill, intelligence, longevity, or wealth; it's about character. And when I read an obituary that says, "Above all, she will be remembered for being a channel of well-being, peace, and joy" or "God was so transparently at work in his life that you felt, if you stayed close to him, you'd keep close to God," I think, "I'll have one of those, please. I'd like an obituary like that, thank you very much."

Would your last paragraph say that about you? Would it say, "She was a channel of well-being, peace, and joy"? Would it say, "God was so transparently at work in his life that you felt, if you stayed close to him, you'd keep close to God"? If not, why not? And with the time God has left for you, what are you going to do about it?

In the end, all the earned or honorary degrees you receive, the money you make or give away, the property you own or bequeath, and even the marriages you enter and the children you have aren't going to matter—at least not in the way that this matters. Others will know if you've received a blessing if they can look back and say that you've been a channel of well-being, peace, and joy to them—that in you, they have found a blessing; that, close to you, they have felt themselves close to God. That's a call to *every* person, and it's the only prosperity God's interested in. If you have that kind of blessing, you don't need any other kind of security. That's something to be named—and something to be claimed. Are you a channel of well-being, peace, and joy? Do you *want* to be? Do you want to receive God's blessing? Does anything else *matter*?

Some questions answer themselves.

# 4

## So Much for Servant Ministry

Recently I met a lively young teenager who'd just received some bad news. She was facing up to the reality that the crutches that she'd been leaning heavily on since an accident fifteen months ago might need to be supporting her for life. She'd gotten involved in a prank that ended with her falling out of a moving vehicle and getting her ankle crushed. We were standing beside each other in a buffet line for dinner, and I quickly realized she needed her hands to hold her crutches, so she had no hands free to fix her dinner plate and carry it, along with her napkin, silverware, and sweet tea, to her table. She was going to need me to do all that. In that moment I had a vision of what her life had turned into, and all the simple details that were now proving immense obstacles. I said to her, "How on earth do you manage with the crutches and all the inconvenience?" She simply replied, without an ounce of self-pity, "You get used to it. You can get used to almost anything after a while."

You can get used to almost anything after a while. It's true. You find coping mechanisms, support networks, carefully honed techniques, and places to take out your frustration. Somehow you adapt to the new normal.

And that makes it easier to understand how we get used to the fact that we had the Lord of Glory in our midst and we contrived to crucify him. You'd think that would be a fact we'd never get used to. It's hard to imagine how any coping mechanisms, support networks, or carefully honed techniques would equip us to come to terms with that particular fact. But we're a pretty resilient bunch, and we really can get used to anything after a while, even that. In fact, we get so good at it that we wrap around it a whole parcel of convictions that make us feel pretty good about Jesus's death and insulate us from most of the truths it tells us and most of the consequences it implies for us.

This accommodation is never more apparent, and its self-serving smugness never more uncomfortable, than in Jesus's actions in the Gospel of John when he gets up from the table after supper, takes off his outer robe, wraps a towel around himself, pours water into a basin, and begins to wash the disciples' feet (John 13:1–20). John gives us two unmistakable signals that this activity is to be understood as the definitive symbolic summary of Jesus's entire mission. First, John 13:1 says, "Having loved his own . . . he loved them to the end." The word *end* is deliberately ambiguous here. It means "end" in the sense of final purpose or goal. But it also means "end" in the sense of "conclusion," as in "the end of the story." Both meanings are significant. This last supper with its meal and foot washing is the conclusion *and* purpose of the story. In other words, "Pay attention. We've got to the important bit. You want to know what Jesus is all about? You're about to find out."

The second signal is that, in his account of Jesus washing the disciples' feet, John offers us a summary of Jesus's whole life. Jesus gets up from the table, takes off his robe, and puts on a towel. In other words, he leaves heaven (the table), puts aside his trappings of divinity (the robe), and takes human form (the towel). He faces controversy from Peter, just as he faces controversy in his ministry. He offers teaching and prophecy, just as in the gospel story. He asks questions and provides an example, just as he does in Galilee and on his journey to Jerusalem. Then he resumes his robe and returns to the table, just as he will return to heaven and be reclothed in the divine mantle.

This succinct highlight reel of the gospel story indicates that the foot washing is a summary of what Jesus is all about. And perhaps as much as any story in the Gospels, the foot-washing story separates those who have come to a more or less happy accommodation with the fact that we've killed the Lord of Glory from those that have not. Let me explain.

Here's the gospel we *want* to believe, the gospel that accommodates this foot-washing story very adeptly indeed. We go off and live the lives we would have lived anyway, but we're free from existential angst about what happens when we die because Jesus assures us of life after death. Jesus makes no particular claim upon our lifestyles other than that we keep our promises and honor those who deserve honor and respect from us. We look to the foot-washing story and say, "You know, it's good to be humble. By all means go and be a big shot in business, industry, medicine, or education, but it's good to give something back, think about the little guy, help out at the night shelter, read to the first grader, or raise money for the struggling nonprofit. And I like to see a senior pastor who does the same, and stays behind after the revival event to clear the chairs away now and again or washes the dishes after the potluck lunch."

We have a name for this philosophy: *service*. We speak of servant leadership or servant ministry. We admire the way Jesus, who was a very busy man after all, and quite senior—maybe he didn't get the salary some people get paid these days, but as Son of God, you've got to say he was in a pretty high-status position—sets such a good example of the philosophy that however senior you are, it's good to put in a good bit of service.

So this is the gospel we want to hear. Jesus doesn't change our lives significantly; in fact he affirms them, because he gave his life to make sure we don't have to give ours, and our way of showing a little gratitude and humility now and again is to give a little back and get down on our knees and do a little foot washing, at least in a figurative way.

As the young woman on the crutches said to me, "You get used to it. You can get used to almost anything after a while." This is how we've got used to Jesus's astonishing action at the Last Supper. We've found a tidy way to accommodate it in a benevolent gospel of personal development and modest social service.

But is that really the gospel? Don't get me wrong—I'm all for reading to elementary schoolchildren and serving at night shelters, and I firmly believe Jesus will say, "Whatever you did to the least of these you did unto me." But is this the high-water mark of the radical claims of the Christian gospel? I'm not sure it is.

So this is the gospel we *don't* want to hear. In John 13 Jesus gets down on his knees and washes the disciples' feet. Just a chapter earlier Mary of Bethany gets down on her knees and washes Jesus's feet with her hair. There are plenty of reasons why what she's doing is scandalous—the perfume is a terrible waste of money and the erotic intimacy of the action is wholly inappropriate. But Jesus praises Mary for one single reason. *She alone has realized that Jesus is about to die.* She is washing his feet to prepare his body for burial. Now here we are, just one chapter later. And it's a second foot-washing scene. The gospel we *want* urges us to read this as a lesson in humility, in servant leadership. But God isn't interested in the gospel we want. The gospel in front of us says, this foot-washing scene means pretty much exactly what the first foot-washing scene meant. Jesus is saying, "Mary prepared me to die. Now I'm preparing *you* to die."

See how this reading makes sense of the several curious statements uttered in this chapter. Peter says to Jesus, "You will never wash my feet" (John 13:8a). Fair enough. Peter doesn't want to die. Who can blame him? Peter's simply expressing what we all feel. We love Jesus until the moment he asks us to die. Then we say, "Enough's enough." But listen to Jesus's reply in the light of what we can now see foot washing to mean: "Jesus answered, 'Unless I wash you, *you have no share with me*'" (John 13:8b, emphasis added). In other words, unless you are willing to die with me, you can't expect to share in my resurrection. Then Peter blunders on, "Lord, not my feet only but also my hands and my head!" (John 13:9).

This is the most difficult part of the story to understand. But it all falls into place if we realize what's going on is a distinction between foot washing and baptism. Jesus reinforces this when he replies, "One who has bathed does not need to wash, except for the feet, but is entirely clean" (John 13:10). He's talking about baptism. Baptism prepares us for life—but foot washing prepares us for death. Peter is saying, "Wash me all over, Jesus. Baptize me again, by all means." Jesus is saying, "No, Peter, you've *been* baptized. You've fundamentally passed over from death to life. You don't need to be baptized again. All that needs washing right now is your feet. And that's because washing feet is preparing you to die. Washing feet is inviting you to face the full consequences of your baptism." That's what Jesus means when he says, "One who has bathed does not need to wash, except for the feet, but is entirely clean." You only need baptism once, but you need foot washing pretty frequently. Otherwise baptism becomes something you find a way of getting used to.

Let's keep going a little further in the story and see what Jesus says when he returns to the table. He says, "You call me Teacher and Lord—and you are right, for that is what I am" (John 13:13). Now this doesn't fit with the humble service interpretation at all. Humble servants don't go around saying this kind of thing. They play down hierarchies and use words like *colleague* rather than *boss*—let alone *Lord*. Jesus is quite clear he's the boss. Which means he gets to say, "If I, your Lord and Teacher, have washed your feet, you also ought to wash one another's feet" (John 13:14). In other words, if I have been preparing you to face death, *you need to get into the habit of preparing one another for death.*

Here, then, are two fundamental moments in our Christian life. Baptism is the beginning, the moment when we pass from death to life, the moment when the power of death ceases to dominate our imaginations. And foot washing is the end, the moment when we are prepared to face death, the moment when we help one another face the consequences of our baptism.

Have you washed any feet lately? Have you prepared anyone for death? Have you helped anyone face the true consequences of their baptism? Has anyone done that for you?

None of us, deep down, really want to hear this gospel. We want church to be about making friends, feeling spiritual, and offering service. We don't really want it to be about preparing one another for death.

Jesus speaks the truth. The truth takes him to the cross. Why? Because he is an agent of reconciliation and witness in the face of oppression and of communities who make a travesty of God. He calls us to follow him. He says, simply and unambiguously, "I have set you an example, that you also should do as I have done to you" (John 13:15). And if we do indeed follow him, quite plainly, we shall go to the cross too. For the first disciples that meant nails and wood and asphyxiation and agony. For us it may mean being humiliated and defamed in newspapers, blogs, and radio stations. It may mean losing our jobs, and we and those who love us becoming the objects of scorn and derision. It may mean being subject to violence against our person, property, and loved ones. It may mean imprisonment or restrictions on travel, speech, or education. This is what happens to people when they spend their lives devoted to reconciliation, healing, truth, and Jesus.

We don't want that gospel. We want the servant ministry thing instead. It's much nicer. But Jesus wants to wash our feet. He's been preparing for death for a while. It's time for him to prepare us. The question for us is, are we ready to start preparing? Jesus is kneeling before us because he loves us to the end. Do we want what he wants? Do we want Jesus? Do we love him? Will we love to the end? Will we? Really?

# 5

# The Five Ws

I remember where I was and what I was doing. I was sitting with my older sister in the TV room in the house where we grew up. We were hurling cushions at each other, with a mixture of idleness, playfulness, and savagery, as children do. I was about eight years old. And that was the moment, just then, in the dizziness of being struck by a flying sofa cushion, that I had, for the first time, a sudden realization: "I am going to die." The terrifying thought swept over me, obscuring all other sensation. I didn't burst into tears, because tears seemed pointless. Tears are a call for help, and I had a deep sense that there wasn't anyone who could help. What horrified me about death was the blankness of isolation, of being eternally alone in a whiteout of unconsciousness. My sister noticed I'd stopped throwing the cushions back, and said, "What's the matter?" I replied, monosyllabically, "One day I'm going to die." And my sister looked straight back at me and said, with gentle eyes, "Yes, we all are." And then I was dumbfounded again. How could she know this and still be able to idle time away throwing cushions?

Some while later it began to dawn on me that death might not involve nothingness. It might involve pain—the agony of pain inflicted on me and the guilt of all the pain I'd inflicted on others.

And so eventually, in my stumbling way, I arrived at the four great fears that strike all of us from time to time and strike most of us overwhelmingly for short or long periods: death, pain, guilt, and isolation. At some point all of us are like little children, surrounded by pelted cushions, who've just discovered the truth about the world. Death, pain, guilt, and isolation. These are the profound and justified fears that can bring us to our knees, yearning for a word of hope to encourage and sustain us.

And that word of hope comes from deep in the bowels of time, from the prophet Isaiah, writing in exile in Babylon 2,500 years ago. Why are the prophet Isaiah's words, written so long ago, so far away, with clothes and customs and assumptions and attitudes we most of the time think we've long grown out of, so significant? Because Babylon, to an Israelite like Isaiah, was the end of the world. Babylon was the epitome of death, pain, guilt, and isolation. Death, because it seemed the dream of the Promised Land had died. Pain, because anyone who planned a renaissance for the Jews was going to be in big trouble. Guilt, because exile was a tragedy Israel had brought upon itself. And isolation, because Israel was like a teaspoon of sugar, and Babylon was like a huge cup of tea inexorably dissolving each granule until there was nothing left.

You could say this is the moment when the Christian faith begins. If Christianity is what emerges from seeing how God takes God's love for Israel and makes it a gift for the whole world, then this moment, with Israel facing death, pain, guilt, and isolation in exile, is where that faith begins. This is a nation in deep depression. This is the moment when Israel hits the very bottom. And so now let's see what the prophet Isaiah brings to a people who are disintegrating as fast and as irreversibly as a teaspoon of dissolving sugar.

Isaiah uses a technique that, if he were a modern-day journalist, he'd call the Five Ws. Back in the days before cable TV, the internet, and blogs, we used to have a profession called journalism. The Five Ws are a checklist journalists once used to ensure their information-gathering was comprehensive. The Five Ws are the five questions you need to answer to have a good handle on any situation. Where? What? Who? When? and Why? In the first seven verses of his forty-third chapter, Isaiah sets about a comprehensive information-gathering exercise on Israel in exile. And his Five Ws take the nation in a few short verses from the deep depression of death, pain, guilt, and isolation to the hope that anticipates the Christian gospel.

Isaiah declares:

> But now thus says the LORD,
>   he who created you, O Jacob,
>   he who formed you, O Israel:
> Do not fear, for I have redeemed you;
>   I have called you by name, you are mine.
> When you pass through the waters, I will be with you;
>   and through the rivers, they shall not overwhelm you;
> when you walk through fire you shall not be burned,
>   and the flame shall not consume you.
> For I am the LORD your God,
>   the Holy One of Israel, your Savior.
> I give Egypt as your ransom,
>   Ethiopia and Seba in exchange for you.
> Because you are precious in my sight,
>   and honored, and I love you,
> I give people in return for you,
>   nations in exchange for your life.
> Do not fear, for I am with you;
>   I will bring your offspring from the east,
>   and from the west I will gather you;
> I will say to the north, "Give them up,"
>   and to the south, "Do not withhold;
> bring my sons from far away
>   and my daughters from the end of the earth—
> everyone who is called by my name,
>   whom I created for my glory,
>   whom I formed and made." (Isa. 43:1–7)

First, Isaiah says to Israel, "*Where* are you?" It sounds like a silly question. The obvious answer is, "We're in exile, a thousand miles from home, under an oppressive regime, facing extinction as a people and oblivion as a nation." But Isaiah says, "You are in the world God created. You're not just anywhere in space, floating aimlessly in a vast emptiness. You're in a world that God has personally formed and made, you're in a place that God has explicitly designed and shaped, you're in a very precise place, and most importantly you're at the very center of God's concentrated gaze. You may feel like you're at the back of beyond, but in fact you're at the heart of it all. That's *where* you are."

Before Israel can furrow its brow in dismissive disbelief, Isaiah goes on to his second question. "Israel, *what* are you?" Again, the answer seems obvious. "We're a bunch of biblical has-beens, a rejected spare part of God's shelved providential project." But Isaiah says, "There are three words that sum up what you are: *precious*, *honored*, and *loved*. You're *precious* to God, because you're at the very center of God's purposes. That's as precious as precious can be. You're *honored* by God, because God has made you crucial to God's vision for the whole creation. That's a place of incredible honor. And you're *loved* by God. In other words God doesn't see you as some kind of means to a further end; God doesn't *use* you as an instrument to some wider good, an instrument that can be just tossed away when it breaks or fails or God loses interest in it. God cares about you for your own sake, studies you intimately, knows you wholly and truly, and will never lose sight of you. Precious, honored, and loved. That's *what* you are."

"Okay," Israel may be thinking, "we're getting the hang of this." But Isaiah has plenty more to say. "Israel, *who* are you?" Israel is ready with a quick answer: "We're God's ex—we're the rejected lover, the dumped partner, the embarrassing skeleton in God's cupboard." But Isaiah says, "You're mistaking God's anger for a lack of love. Indifference is a sign of lack of love. God isn't indifferent to you. God's angry with you. Anger is a sign of love, a sign of hurt love. God has not rejected you—you've rejected God, and God desperately wants you back. This is who God is. God is the Lord your God, the Holy One of Israel, your Savior. Do you hear those words? *Your* God, *of Israel*, *your* Savior. You are part of God's name. You're integral to God's identity. God has made you part of who God is. And God calls you by name. That's the first thing God says to you. 'I have redeemed you; I have called you by name. You are mine.' God has made you part of God's very identity. So your identity is in God. The answer to the question, 'Who are you?' lies in the question, '*Whose* are you?' And this is God's answer: 'You are mine, Israel. That's *who* you are. You belong to me.'"

You can almost feel the muscles relaxing in Israel's disbelieving face, the tension of exile beginning to be transformed by the yearning poetry of God. Isaiah goes on, "Israel, *when* are you?" Israel knows these are not the good times. The obvious answer is, "We're on a tiny island waiting for the tsunami finally to obliterate us. We're locked in a burning building waiting to be totally consumed by the flames." But God says through Isaiah, "When you pass through the waters, I'll be with you; and through the rivers, they shall not overwhelm you; when you walk through fire you shall not be burned, and the flame shall not consume you." Notice it doesn't say, "You won't find yourself in deep water; you won't walk through fire." Isaiah knows that's right where Israel is, and there's no use pretending otherwise. But that's the point. The promise is not, "You won't face death, pain, guilt, isolation. You won't face flaming fire and flooding water." The promise is, "*When* you face these things, they won't destroy you, they won't drown you, they won't overwhelm you, they won't fundamentally separate you from me." Isaiah recognizes the bad news about *when* Israel is. Israel is at the worst moment of its life. But Isaiah brings good news. "This is as bad as it gets, and this hasn't and won't destroy you or obliterate you or separate you from God."

And then there's one more W. Isaiah asks, "Israel, *why* are you?" In other words, "What's it all about, Israel? What's the meaning of your existence? *Why* are you?" Here we're at the root of Israel's despair, maybe our own despair. What's the meaning of life? It's a big question, maybe the biggest of all. But Isaiah isn't daunted by it. God's answer lies in three unambiguous words: "For my glory." Faced with the unrelenting threat of our own death, pain, guilt, and isolation, we human beings understandably strive to make our own meaning, carve our own memorial, leave our own mark on the world. We create organizations, build edifices, have and raise children, invent products, devise theories, endow institutions, break records—all to stave off the ravages of time and hold back onrushing oblivion. But the truth is, there's only one thing that's eternal: God's glory. Everything else is dust and ashes. What Isaiah is saying is, "Look, here's the miracle: God has invested God's glory in *you*. That's the only thing on which you can rest any hope. And that is enough. That's the meaning of existence. To be a theater for God's glory. And the amazing grace of God is this. God has made you part of the show."

Those are the Five Ws that Isaiah gives Israel to reappraise and reassess its situation in the midst of exile.

- You're not far away; you're at the heart of it all.
- You're not a has-been; you're precious, honored, and loved.
- You're not rejected; you belong to God.
- You *are* in the fire, but God's right in there with you.
- Your life isn't pointless; it's a reflection of God's glory.

But there's one crucial question, for the journalist and the believer, that doesn't begin with a W. For a Christian, it's the question that turns Isaiah's words from a promise into a reality. And it begins with an H. How? "*How* will all this happen? How will we know? How can we trust?"

Isaiah doesn't answer that question. We find the answer to that question in the Gospel of Luke, in the account of Jesus's baptism. Jesus is baptized by John at the Jordan. The heaven opens, the Holy Spirit descends as a dove, and the voice says, "You are my Son, the Beloved; with you I am well pleased" (Luke 3:22). Here every W question finds its fulfillment. *Where* are we? At the waters, the formless waters of creation, the parting waters of the Red Sea, the waters of the Jordan that Israel crossed to enter the Promised Land. We're at God's new beginning. That's where we are. *What* are we? We're God's children, that's what. *Who* are we? We're God's beloved, that's who we are. *When* are we? Well, John's just spoken of fire, and here we are in the water. We're at a moment when we're terrified by the heat of the fire and the tidal wave of the water and yet we're at the very moment when the heavens open and the dove comes down to say God's right in it with us. *Why* are we? We exist for the glory of God—and look, at this precise second God's glory is fulfilled, and God is well pleased.

There are the Five Ws, and they all culminate in the final question, How? And the answer—the how—is Jesus. Isaiah dismantles Israel's despair and depression with five Ws, and God fulfills all five Ws in the all-important how. Jesus is that how. Jesus is the way God brings God's people home from exile; the way God shows them they're precious, honored, and loved; the way God calls them by name; the way God walks with them through fire and flood; the way God displays God's glory. Jesus is the reason we trust in God. Jesus is God's word of hope to us in our exile of death, pain, guilt, and isolation.

32

Sometimes I still feel like I'm eight years old. Sometimes I feel like all the thrashings and strivings of my life are no more than a pointless sibling fight with tailored sofa cushions. Sometimes—quite often in fact—I still feel transfixed with the realization, "One day I'm going to die, and I could face endless pain, eternal guilt, or isolated oblivion." But Isaiah stands before me, still and steady like my sister did all those years ago, holds my gaze, and says gently, tenderly, truly, "Yes, we all are. We're all going to die. But God isn't. That's the point. Your life has no meaning, no purpose, no lasting significance, except in this: God has made you God's precious beloved, God has shaped God's identity around you, God is with you in fire and rain, and you will live forever as a song to God's glory." That's my only hope. And that is enough.

# PART 2

# be not afraid of weakness

There are two dimensions of discipleship. One is the learning of habits and the forming of character, the shaping of commitments and the inscribing of rhythms, the training in disciplines and the facing of sacrifices. Some people speak as if that were the only part. But the other dimension is perhaps even more important. It is the acknowledgment of weakness, the asking for help, the naming of failure, the request for forgiveness, the desire for reconciliation, and the longing for restoration.

If we knew the truth about one another we would talk a lot more about the second than the first. But while the first inspires a confident proclamation, the second needs a tender application. The person seeking to articulate the Christian gospel in the face of fear must expect that God will be at least as visible and tangible in weakness as in strength—if not more so. For all the widespread insistence that the church has a different message from the world, this conviction—that God is made known in weakness more than in strength—is perhaps the sharpest daily distinction.

And yet it is one Christian congregations find so hard to believe, to embody, and to anticipate. Things will go wrong—faith will falter, clarity will fog, pastors will have feet of clay, congregation members will quarrel, long and sad periods will descend, relationships will fail, children will go astray, temptation will sometimes prove irresistible. The Bible is full of such things. So is the church. So should any account of the gospel be. These need not be the moments when discipleship ends. These may be the moments when it begins.

# 6

# Is There a Balm in Gilead?

A friend of mine taught public school after leaving college. For fifteen years he was successful and popular and all was well, until about eight years ago when he was struck down by a mystery illness that's left him unable to work and permanently fatigued. Everyone he's ever met thinks they have a cure for him, usually because they had a nephew who had a similar thing, or because they believe in acupuncture, vitamins, or scratching your left toe with your right ear when the clock strikes four. With amazing courtesy and patience, he gently says to each one, "Yes, thank you, that's very thoughtful and helpful, but I've actually tried that remedy and it doesn't seem to work for me." He's had stronger periods and times of desperate weakness, but, eight years on, things are more or less the same. One day I asked him, "What do you really think has happened to you?" He replied, "I've passed from the kingdom of the well to the kingdom of the sick. I now live in a different world. People like me who have a long-term, severe, or terminal illness pass into a different realm, where time is different, and emotions are different, and intimacy is different, and food is different, and somehow even sound is different. I call it the kingdom of the sick."[1]

---

1. For the whole story, see David Trelawny-Ross, *A Dream of White Horses: Surviving and Making Sense of an Experience of Illness* (Raleigh, NC: Lulu.com, 2008).

The kingdom of the sick. I wonder if you've spent any time there, maybe with a family member, maybe on your own. Maybe you're there right now, in that different realm, in a different time, with different food and different feelings. The threshold between the kingdom of the well and the kingdom of the sick is fraught with anxiety and the most profound emotions. Many of us, when we find ourselves with terrible headaches, constant diarrhea, a strange growth under one arm, disturbing chest pains, or unaccountable dizziness, have a fear lurking at the back of our minds that this may not be a simple thing; this may be the start of something major, something that could change our whole identity.

And quickly a whole host of negative and derogatory words begin to cluster around. "I don't want to be a burden," "I'm becoming a basket case," "I'm turning into a loser." We're fighting the pain or fear, but perhaps even more we're fighting the transition we dread to make into the kingdom of the sick, because entering the kingdom of the sick is a devastating loss of control, a kind of death.

That's the threshold the prophet Jeremiah is crossing in his description in Jeremiah 8 of the gradual descent of his people into the whirlpool of defeat, invasion, humiliation, and exile in the sixth century BC. He's seen all the symptoms: the armies have gathered, the people haven't learned their lesson, the battles have been lost, the fall of Jerusalem is simply a matter of time. There's only one way this is going: Judah is dying. The dream of the Promised Land is about to be snuffed out. Jeremiah is devastated. In Jeremiah 8:18–21 he says, "My joy is gone, grief is upon me, my heart is sick. . . . 'The harvest is past, the summer is ended, and we are not saved.' . . . For the hurt of my poor people I am hurt, I mourn, and dismay has taken hold of me." In other words, I can't pretend anymore that there's a good outcome here.

I vividly remember going to visit someone I loved very much who had been suffering from a mysterious illness for several months. When I went to see her in the hospital she looked terrible—far worse than I expected. She wasn't that much older than me (and this was ten years ago when I was still a spring chicken). Unreality seemed to have gripped the whole family. No one could name what was happening. I said to her mother-in-law, "Has anyone faced the fact that she isn't going to get any better? Why can't anyone see it?" And a week later

38

she was dead. No one in her life, herself included, could face the truth that she'd passed over into the kingdom of the sick—still less the fact that she wasn't coming back.

Jeremiah at this moment is just letting the truth cover his face like the rays of the rising sun. But it's hard. It's so hard. It's not just that he's losing his city, his people, his future. It's that everything Jeremiah knows, most of all God himself, is wrapped up in the destiny of Jerusalem. God's covenant is shaped around Israel's Promised Land. In losing Jerusalem, Jeremiah fears he's losing God altogether. Jeremiah is like a drowning man clinging to the side of the sinking boat and finally realizing there's no use but simply to let go of the rope and be engulfed by the waves.

Is there no balm in Gilead? This is Jeremiah's question. It's one of a string of questions Jeremiah fires out like a hail of arrows as he tries to comes to terms with what's happening to him and to Jerusalem. "Isn't the Lord here?" he asks; "Isn't Israel's king in Jerusalem?" In other words, this is an unthinkable affront to God's honor. It cannot be. Then he says in dismay, "The summer is ended, and we are not saved." If this was some kind of attempt to teach us a lesson, it's got beyond a joke. This has got completely out of control. And then the most famous words, "Is there no balm in Gilead? Is there no physician there?" (Gilead is the region on the east bank of the Jordan.) Can't we just go and find someone who can solve this problem? Surely someone can save us, can make things better, can tell us it's all a bad dream?

This is what it's like to see the one you love capsizing slowly into oblivion. You go through a whole range of rational and irrational attempts to make sense of and correct and somehow come to terms with what's taking place before your eyes. Jeremiah's despair at the demise of Jerusalem is like a parent watching a beloved child die. It's the worst possible nightmare, and it seems to extinguish everything that makes life good and beautiful and true. The novelist Peter De Vries, in his 1961 novel *The Blood of the Lamb*, describes the heart-searchings of a young man called Don Wanderhope. Wanderhope doesn't wander in hope. On the contrary, he wanders in growing despair as he loses his brother, then his wife, and finally, slowly and agonizingly, realizes his only child, Carol, is dying from leukemia at the age of eleven. Don watching Carol die is like Jeremiah watching

Jerusalem fall to the Chaldeans. He goes through all Jeremiah's emotions and more. Surveying the other dying children in the hospital, many even worse off than his daughter, Carol, Don rages at God, saying God is like Herod in the Christmas story, plotting the slaughter of the innocents.

Fleetingly Don tries to look on the bright side, and says philosophically to a fellow parent that medical research has given their children a chance they'd never have had ten years before. But the other parent is having none of it. "So death by leukemia is now a local instead of an express. Same run, only a few more stops. But that's medicine. The art of prolonging disease." "Why would anyone want to prolong it?" asks Don. "In order to postpone grief," comes the reply.[2] There is no balm in Gilead.

Eleven-year-old Carol has taken up short-term but irreversible residence in the kingdom of the sick. The only thing that would be different about the story today is that Don would spend every night relentlessly scouring the internet for an obscure remedy or neglected research study, and Carol would set up a blog to give her school friends daily updates. The whole tragedy seems unendurable. But suddenly the story takes a new twist. Carol goes into remission, and Don enters the happiest days of his life. He describes what he calls the greatest of all human experiences: the rediscovery of the commonplace. He could read to Carol without a shadow falling across the page, the shadow that this might be one of their last times. He could feel the bliss of finishing an evening with a game of rummy and a mug of cocoa together. It seems there is a balm in Gilead, after all. But the joy is brief. The next test reveals an elevated white blood count, and Don faces utter despair. It seems there is no balm in Gilead after all. For him and for Carol, the future is a thing of the past.

These are the writhings of being with a child as her life descends into a spiral of multisyllabled drugs and furrow-browed professionals. It takes the caring loved one into the most extraordinary and distressing mental and emotional territory. I recall a young woman called Kirsty wandering from table to table in a hospital restaurant. Her boyfriend had more or less destroyed his own liver, and he urgently needed a transplant to survive. Kirsty was beside herself and

2. Peter De Vries, *The Blood of the Lamb* (Boston: Little, Brown, 1961), 182–83.

sought out the most elderly people in the restaurant. To each one she said, tearfully, "My boyfriend could use a new liver upstairs on ward 43 right now. Are you sure you need your liver more than he needs it?" The true horror dawned on them when they looked into her wild and pleading eyes and realized she really meant it.

Sometimes the search for balm in Gilead can become as frenzied and desperate as that. But other times it can be exhausting and utterly confusing. As a teenager I watched my mother die of cancer over three long years. In the last month she reached the point where she was so thin, frail, and ghostly that it was uncomfortable even to look at her. For two weeks after she finally died I had a recurring dream in which she'd come back to life and I wouldn't want her to. I would gently but firmly lie her back down again and say, "No, really, please, it's much easier if you just die now." I would wake up wracked with guilt, but after a few months I was able to let go. I realized the dreams were more than anything a sign that I'd reached my emotional limit. I was a kid, I was out of my depth, and I couldn't endure the kingdom of the sick any longer.

Is there a balm in Gilead? Is there any hope in the face of terminal illness? Is there anything left to say to a dying child or her parents? Jeremiah adds a whole extra dimension to this question in what he tells us next. The series of questions, writhings, and searchings for remission, salve, or cure finally gives way to a convulsive outpouring of tears. "O that my head were a spring of water, and my eyes a fountain of tears, so that I might weep day and night for the slain of my poor people!" (Jer. 9:1). But here's the absorbing discovery. It's not clear who's doing the crying. The question, "Is there no balm in Gilead?" is coming from Jeremiah, but what follows the tears are the words of God. It's as if in the tears, God's grief intermingles with Jeremiah's lament and transfigures it.

This is the center of the Christian faith, but it's somehow so difficult to grasp. We have hardwired into us the sense that God is angry with us, that we're fundamentally clumsy children and we're always on the edge of waking the sleepy but obstreperous, heavily bearded divine grandfather. We're like Don Wanderhope, knowing his beloved daughter is past the point where medicine can help, but still looking to the physicians with a mixture of yearning and fury, and seeing God beyond them as a physician on a massive scale, yet

41

one who is either hostile or negligent. "Is there a balm in Gilead?" we ask, in a pleading yet increasingly furious voice, because there *must* be—it's just a question of whether God the weary pharmacist can be bothered to let us have it.

But the center of the Christian faith is that God is not the idle physician that Don Wanderhope despairs of. God is not the weary pharmacist impervious to our distress. God is Carol. God in Jesus becomes the dying child. That's the story of our salvation. God's tears mingle with our tears, the way Carol's tears mingle with her father's. This is the balm in Gilead. It's not a soothing, comforting balm, necessarily. A lot of the time we'd prefer the sleepy, bearded grandfather to be angry with, because in his majesty and might there's always the possibility he could stretch down a weary hand and set us straight.

But that's not who God in Christ shows himself to be. God in Christ appears to us as Carol. God, in Jesus, enters the kingdom of the sick. God is dying to be with us. We are exhausted, exasperated, and emptied out by the truth, but it turns out God is closer to the truth than we are. God isn't a distant, heartless observer; he's actually inside the pain. When we cry for our dying child, we're sharing the grief of God for his dying child. Our tears mingle with God's tears. We are never closer to God than at this moment. *That's* the balm in Gilead.

And how do we reach Gilead? Remember, Gilead lies beyond the River Jordan. That's where God meets us. The waters of the Jordan are made up of the tears of God, blended with the tears of all our grieving. The journey to Gilead crosses that river of tears. It's the journey we call baptism. That's what baptism is: being bathed, healed, cleansed, and renewed in the waters that flow from the broken heart of God. *That's* the balm in Gilead. The tears of the living God. The tears that make up the water of our baptism. To be baptized in the tears of God: this is the truest balm of all.

There is a balm in Gilead. There is. But you can only see it through your tears. Through God's tears.

# 7

# The Hound of Heaven

I once knew a young woman who told me, "I get so angry with the Bible!" When I asked why, she said that her husband, who was new to Christianity, often had friends round for an evening, and one or two of them would pick up a Bible and open it randomly and read out an obscure passage and just laugh at how strange it sounded. For those of us who've been led to believe that the Bible is a good commonsense guide for living, the young woman's anger is understandable. Many of us have been led to believe, like her, that the Bible is fundamentally about us, and so of course it should speak to us straightforwardly in language we can understand.

But the truth is the Bible is not fundamentally about us. The Bible is fundamentally about God. And our efforts to translate the truth about God into more or less useful guides for living are never anything other than provisional, and certainly never as tidy as we would like. Take the beginning of Luke 15. Luke 15:1 says, "Now all the tax collectors and sinners were coming near to listen to him." Jesus is surrounded by tax collectors and sinners—in other words, people whose style of life made them ritually unclean and morally reprehensible. The one thing Israel was called to be above all was holy—remembering the words of Leviticus 20:26, "You shall be holy to me; for I the Lord am holy." This was the aim of the Pharisees—to make sure, in the minutest particulars, that all the people of Israel were holy. There was no way in the world that the tax collectors and sinners could be holy, so the Pharisees and the scribes said that if this Jesus were truly of God, truly holy, he'd be keeping well away from them.

And then Jesus tells these two stories. If a shepherd has one hundred sheep, and one goes missing, surely he would leave the ninety-nine and go after the one that was lost; and then, having found the lost sheep, he would lay the animal on his shoulders and rejoice; and on returning home he would have a great party with his friends and neighbors. Likewise, if a woman has ten silver coins, and one goes missing, surely she would search her house without pause until she found it; and on discovering the coin, she would have a great party with her friends and neighbors.

Now when we read these stories, tuned in as we are to assuming the Bible is saying something about us, we may think to ourselves, "Well, there sure are some pretty bad people out there. Some of them have made a hefty profit out of sin, like the tax collectors, and others have doubtless hurt themselves as much as anyone else and just ended up making a mess of their lives, like the people Luke calls sinners. But I guess we should be generous and broad-minded and care about those whom others might look down on. We should be shepherds who search out the lost; we should be careful householders who treasure each and every coin." And so we become people who do good. One Irish writer describes such a woman in these words: "She's the sort of woman who lives for others—you can always tell the others by their hunted expression."[1] In short we become patrons—people who, out of our generosity, deign to give a hand up to a person in need.

But becoming patrons is not what these parables are about. These stories are not fundamentally about us. These stories are fundamentally about God. Jesus isn't just calling the Pharisees to be a bit more generous—he is calling them to repentance, a complete reversal of their way of seeing and being in the world. They grumble over time wasted on the disreputable when they

1. C. S. Lewis, *The Screwtape Letters* (New York: HarperCollins, 2001), 145.

should be wild with joy at the way God seeks out and finds these precious, lost treasures. The point of these two parables is not for us to identify with the shepherd and the woman. We are not the shepherd; we are the lost sheep. We are not the woman; we are the lost coin. God is the shepherd; God is the searching woman. God is the one who takes the astonishing risk of leaving the ninety-nine sheep and coming to look for us, a journey of danger, daring, and devotion, a journey we could call passion. God is the one who carefully, thoughtfully seeks us out like a woman meticulously and methodically tracking down a lost coin.

Jesus is saying, whoever you are, Pharisaic lawmaker or sinful law-breaker, this is not a story about you. It's a story about God. And the way to allow yourself to become part of the story is to stop running away, to stop hiding from the one who yearns and searches for you.

Few people have understood these parables better than Francis Thompson.[2] Thompson was born into a well-to-do Catholic family in Manchester, England, in 1859. He was sent to a boarding school to prepare him for the priesthood. When it became clear his vocation lay elsewhere, he was sent to train, like his father, to be a physician. But his studies made him miserable, and, after the death of his mother, he started to take opium. He came to London at the age of twenty-six and fell into a low life on the streets, facing hunger, disease, and drug addiction. Two years later, he was on the verge of suicide when he was befriended by a prostitute who took him in and cared for him through the winter. Two astonishing events followed. First, the literary editor Wilfred Meynell published one of Thompson's poems, and they began a close friendship that was to endure for the rest of Thompson's life. And second, the prostitute, whose name is not known, recognized that Thompson had found a hitherto unknown peace among his new friends and disappeared from his life. Her last words to him were, "They will not understand our friendship."[3] There is no other word in the Christian vocabulary for the publication of that poem but *providence*, and there are

2. See Paul van Kuykendall Thomson, *Francis Thompson: A Critical Biography* (New York: Thomas Nelson, 1961), especially pages 15–58; and Thomas Marc Parrott, *Poetry of the Transition, 1850–1914*, ed. Thomas Marc Parrott and Willard Thorp (New York: Oxford University Press, 1932), 310–11.

3. Parrott, *Poetry of the Transition*, 310.

no other words in the theological lexicon for the ministry of that prostitute but *Holy Spirit*.

One hundred years ago, shortly before his death, Thompson wrote a poem in which he recognized that all his life he had been running away, and fundamentally the one he had been running away from was not his own father but God. His own life was secondary to the fundamental narrative, which was God's relentless pursuit of him. The celebrated poem is called "The Hound of Heaven."[4] It begins,

> I fled Him, down the nights and down the days;
> I fled Him, down the arches of the years;
> I fled Him, down the labyrinthine ways
> Of my own mind; and in the mist of tears
> I hid from Him.

In the poem, Thompson explains why he was fleeing: he admits,

> though I knew his love who followèd,
> Yet was I sore adread
> Lest, having him, I must have naught beside.

Yet the hound of heaven pursued him with all "deliberate speed." (You might recognize the phrase "all deliberate speed"; it was re-minted in the second Brown v. Board Supreme Court judgment on school desegregation in 1955.) In the end the reader of the poem is less fascinated by the reasons and emotions of the one running away and is instead captivated by the persistence, the relentless pursuit, and most of all the passion of the hound of heaven, the love that will not let Thompson go. The hound of heaven is one and the same with the woman searching for the lost coin and the shepherd search-ing for the stray sheep: each one is God in Christ, who searches us out and knows us, who comes to us in any form we can receive him, even—astonishingly, as for Thompson—in the form of a prostitute, simply because God is the love that will not let us go.

We are not the searchers in Luke's parables: we are the found. God is not the goal of our seeking: God is the hound that tracks us

---

4. Wilfred Meynell, ed., *Francis Thompson: Poems and Essays* (Westminster, MD: The Newman Bookshop, 1947), 107–13.

down however hard and fast we are determined to run away. And if we have discovered the joy of being found, we long to share that joy with others who have made a similar discovery. These new friendships are not ones in which we do the seeking or the finding, but ones in which we experience the joy of being found.

This is a joy perfectly expressed by Vincent Donovan. Father Donovan was a Roman Catholic priest who became exasperated with conventional forms of Catholic education in Tanzania in the 1960s and received permission from his bishop simply to go out among the Masai tribes and share their life and talk about God. There he discovered how to read these two parables as stories not about us but about God. Initially he wrestled with his own doubts about how the particular story of Jesus's cross and resurrection translated into the Masai culture all around him. But a Masai elder converted Donovan by contrasting the faith of a Western hunter with the faith of an African lion. The Masai elder showed Donovan that his notion of faith was a profoundly Western notion. It was merely intellectual assent. "To 'believe' like that was similar to a white hunter shooting an animal with his gun from a great distance. Only his eyes and his fingers took part in the act." The Masai elder said, "For a [person] really to believe is like a male lion going after its prey. His nose and eyes and ears pick up on the prey. His legs give him the speed to catch it. All the power of his body is involved in the terrible death leap and single blow to the neck with the front paw, the blow that actually kills. And as the animal goes down the lion envelops it in his arms, . . . pulls it to itself, and makes it part of himself. This is the way a lion kills. This is the way a [person] believes. This is what faith is."

Hearing this, Donovan understood for the first time why, when his faith was gone, he ached in every fiber of his being. Faith wasn't intellectual assent: it was a whole body experience, outer senses and inner organs. It mattered all over, and, when it was missing, it hurt all over. Remember, we discovered in the first parable we are not the shepherd; we are the sheep. In the second parable we are not the woman; we are the coin. The Masai elder went on in words that echo Luke's two parables. Here is what he had to say to Father Donovan about faith: "You told us of the High God, how we must search for him, even leave our land and our people to find him. But we have not done this. We have not left our land. We have not searched for him. *He has searched for us.* He has searched *us* out and found us. *All the time we think we are the lion. In the end, the lion is God.*"[5]

The lion is God. Here are we, thinking our heart-searchings of faith, our journey, ourselves is what the story is all about. But brothers and sisters, this is the good news: the story is all about God. The lion is God. God is the hound of heaven who searches us out and knows us; God in Christ is the good shepherd who leaves the ninety-nine to come and find us; God in Christ is the woman who cared so much that she set everything aside to find us, her oh-so-precious lost coin. Faith is not a heroic journey: faith is the acceptance of being found.

Francis Thompson tried to be a priest and a physician and ended up as a vagrant. All of these turned out to be different forms of running away from God. Only when he was able to receive real friendship did he stop running away. Vincent Donovan tried to be a teacher to the Masai, but only when he went out among their tribes did he discover what faith really was. May we, like Donovan, find out who the God searching for us really is. May we stop running away. May we make new friends who have discovered, like us, that we are not the lion. The lion is God.

5. Vincent Donovan, *Christianity Rediscovered*, 25th anniversary ed. (Maryknoll, NY: Orbis Books, 2003), 48.

# 8

# Speak Tenderly to Jerusalem

Egypt and Babylon. The Old Testament is shaped around these two stories. First the children of Israel are slaves in Egypt. God raises up Moses and through the exodus brings God's people to freedom in the Promised Land. Then we wait to see what they'll do with their freedom. Then they're in exile in Babylon. There they discover a part of God's character they hadn't known before, and they return with a new understanding of themselves and a new understanding of God. Then we wait to see whether the life they have after their return from Babylon can really be called freedom.

The stories are similar. But there's a big difference between them. Slavery in Egypt is not Israel's fault. They were hungry, so they came to Egypt; they did well there, so they became a threat to the regime; the regime made them slaves to keep them down. So when we imagine Israel in Egypt, we identify with the oppressed everywhere, the downtrodden, abused, hurt, and cruelly treated. We like to read these stories, because it makes us feel righteous. It tells us God vindicates in the face of injustice. God sets history straight.

But Babylon isn't like that. The books of Isaiah, Kings, Jeremiah, Lamentations, and Ezekiel make no mistake in portraying Israel's time in exile as a time of suffering and sorrow. But the difference is that the time in Babylon is *self-inflicted* sorrow. This is suffering that *need not have been*. This is suffering that Israel brought on itself by turning aside from God's ways. We don't like to read these stories. They don't make us feel righteous. They make us feel embarrassed and uncomfortable. We'd rather take refuge in military, economic, and geopolitical explanations for the fall of the Israelite kingdom. But the Bible has none of it. Israel made her own bed and spent seventy years lying in it. That's what it says.

I wonder how that embarrassment and discomfort touches you. I wonder if there's a suffering and pain in your life that need not have been, because it was self-inflicted. Yes, we spend a lot of time licking the wounds of our slavery in Egypt, resenting the ways the sins of others bring us down and make our lives harder than we feel they should be. But I'm not talking about Egypt right now. I'm talking about Babylon. I'm talking about the place you ended up because you got it very badly wrong.

It may be a very visible place, like Babylon was for Israel. It may be that you know what it means to face public humiliation: to hear the gasp of strangers as they've read about you in the paper or sense the anguish of friends or family members (or former friends or family members) who know what you did and feel inconsolably let down. It may be that every time you see certain people you blink and wince because you feel they're judging you for the worst thing you've ever done, and you'll never be able to look them straight in the face again.

Or it may be a secret, known only to you or perhaps one or two others. It may be something you're terrified of coming to light, something you wonder whether you could ever share with anybody without them going cold and distant and politely ending the friendship. You may be wondering if you'll be spending the rest of your life in some kind of hiding or disguise. You may be feeling like you're living in some kind of a prison of your own making, because most of the courses open to you lead to some kind of disclosure, encounter, or reminder that tests the secret to its limit. It could be you find yourself bursting into tears for no reason. Perhaps you're surrounded by people now who couldn't imagine, understand, or ever be reconciled to the story you have to tell. Maybe you feel angry or paralyzed that you have to live your life with this secret chaining you down.

Hear these words of Isaiah: "Comfort, O comfort my people, says your God. Speak tenderly to Jerusalem, and cry to her that she has served her term, that her penalty is paid, that she has received from the LORD's hand double for all her sins" (Isa. 40:1–2). These words are directed at the people of Israel in exile. But I want to look closely at what these words meant to the people of Israel in Babylon to discover precisely what they might mean to us.

Israel has a series of reasons to find God's dazzling new word hard to countenance.

To start with, when we've made a mess of things, when we've sinned big time, there's a lot of hurt. By hurt I mean the impact of wrongdoing on hearts, minds, and souls—and most of all on the heart of God. But besides hurt there's also damage. Damage refers to the lasting practical effects of what we've broken. For Israel the *hurt* was their estrangement from God. The *damage* was the fact that they were in Babylon, a thousand miles from home. But look at what God says. God says, "I'll deal with the hurt *and* the damage." "Cry to Jerusalem that she has served her term, that her penalty is paid." In other words, her sin is forgiven and its consequences are healed. That's the difference between forgiveness and healing. Forgiveness deals with the sin, but after the sin is forgiven there's still the damage to be faced. Healing addresses the damage, and it sometimes takes a whole lot longer.

Israel has another obstacle in the way of accepting God's comfort. "We're thirty days' journey from home, and in between are mountains, valleys, and all sorts of difficult terrain." In other words, I've put myself in such a distant place that even God's forgiveness and healing aren't going to be enough to get me back. Well, this is what God has to say about that distance and that terrain. "Every valley shall be lifted up, and every mountain and hill be made low; the uneven ground shall become level, and the rough places a plain" (Isa. 40:4). In other words, don't you go worrying about the road back. When an ancient Near Eastern king travels around his empire, a herald travels a day or two ahead of him to make sure the road ahead is flat and straight and free of obstacles. That's the way it's going to be for you, Israel—a herald's going ahead of you to make sure your route is all flattened out and well prepared. You're going home on a Blue Ridge Parkway to Zion.

Then there's another obstacle. The flesh is weak. We've had two obstacles that said the damage is too great and the distance too far. Now we've got a third obstacle that says my strength isn't up to it. Israel said, in the old days we had great figures like Jeremiah and Hezekiah. When we came out of Egypt we had Moses. But now they've all gone and we've got no one. We say to ourselves, God may have forgiven me, even healed me, and even overcome the impossibilities of the situation I've created, but I just haven't got it in me to face the future. I'm tired. The grass withers, and I'm like the grass. But this obstacle is dismantled like the previous ones. "The grass withers, the flower fades; but the word of our God will stand for ever" (Isa. 40:8). In other words, you're not going to do this in your own strength. You're going to do this in God's strength. In Isaiah's words from later in the same chapter, "He gives power to the faint, and strengthens the powerless. . . . Those who wait for the LORD shall renew their strength, they shall mount up with wings like eagles, they shall run and not be weary, they shall walk and not faint" (Isa. 40:29, 31).

And then there's yet one more obstacle. And this one seems the biggest of all. We've had one about consequences. We've had another about distance. We've had a third about human weakness. But this last one is the big one. This last one is about fear. Don't forget that Israel assumed that anyone who saw God would die. God was so holy, and Israel felt anything but holy. Remember when Isaiah himself was in the temple in Jerusalem and saw God he was petrified (Isa. 6:1–5). The first three obstacles are about imagining ourselves without this constant burden of guilt and sorrow and regret. It's hard to forgive ourselves because we're used to telling a story in which we're the main player, albeit a player who ruined the play. But even if we can get over our own reservations about being given a new identity free from our sin, we've then got to face up to God. We've got to stop looking at the ground and raise our eyes to meet God's gaze, ashamed as we are.

And here it seems we're in for a big surprise. "Here is your God!" (Isa. 40:9). We're face-to-face with God, and of course we see that God is mighty—God has just overcome our weakness, flattened the mountains and valleys, and repaired all the damage we've done. But it turns out when we look closer that God is really a shepherd who loves us like God's own sheep. Isaiah tells Israel, "[God] will feed his flock like a shepherd; he will gather the lambs in his arms, and carry them in his bosom, and gently lead the mother sheep" (Isa. 40:11). God doesn't drive us faster than we can go, and when the going's too much for us, God gathers us into his arms and carries us in his bosom. Here is your God.

That's how God announces to Israel that her exile is over. God says, "Yes, you sinned, and yes, there've been major consequences, but I've forgiven you and I'm helping you clean up the mess you made. Yes, you've put yourself a long and difficult way from where you should be, but I'll flatten whatever lies between here and there. Yes, you're worn out and in many ways you're as much hurt as those you've hurt, but this is going to be done in my strength, not yours. Yes, sin is a terrible thing in the face of my holiness, but don't be afraid: I love you so tenderly I'll embrace you, and if you can't make the road back alone I'll carry you over the parts where you can't walk."

Think of Isaiah's words as describing a body coming back to life. The first words are about the minerals: rocks, valleys, and rough ground: "Every valley shall be lifted up, and every mountain and hill be laid low" (Isa. 40:4). Then there are words about the vegetation: grass and flowers: "The grass withers, the flower fades; but the word of our God will stand for ever" (Isa. 40:8). Finally there are words about the animals: sheep and lambs: "[God] will feed his flock like a shepherd; he will gather the lambs in his arms" (Isa. 40:11). There's a cosmic coming alive here—the animal, vegetable, and mineral world is coming out of exile too. There's a political coming alive here—Israel is emerging from more than half a century of obscurity and subjugation. And there's a personal coming alive here, as we've just been exploring. Israel's alienation from God has cosmic, political, and personal dimensions and consequences. God resolves these consequences in a cosmic, political, and personal way.

At the center of these words lies this promise. "Then the glory of the Lord shall be revealed, and all flesh shall see it together, for the mouth of the Lord has spoken" (Isa. 40:5). God's solution is so much bigger, so much greater, so much more profound than the problem. Israel had departed from God; after years of grief and sorrow, the result is that *all flesh* shall see God—and live; and the God they shall see is tenderness itself. These words are about Israel coming back to life. That's why they appear at the very beginning of Mark's Gospel. When John the Baptist quotes Isaiah 40:3 and says, "Prepare the way of the Lord" (Mark 1:3), he's saying all these promises are about to come true. Jesus is coming to bring Israel back to life. God the Father is saying to God the Son, "Comfort, O comfort my people. . . . Speak tenderly to Jerusalem, and cry to her that she has served her term, that her penalty is paid" (Isa. 40:1–2).

That's how God announces to Israel that her exile is over. And that's how God announces the same news to you. Maybe you've been carrying this humiliation, embarrassment, secret, or burden that keeps your head down and your eyes focused on the ground in front of you. You know there've been major consequences. But hear this word from God. Comfort ye. You have served your term. Your penalty is paid. It's over. There may be high mountains and deep valleys between you and where you should be, but every one of those valleys shall be exalted, and every one of those mountains and hills shall be made low, and every crooked path shall be made straight, and the rough places be made plain. God is making a straight way for you, a highway to Zion. You may feel so weak that you feel like grass in the wind, but you will be borne up like an eagle on the wings of God's Spirit. And God hasn't utterly forsaken you. God will lead you like a shepherd, and where you can't find it in you to go further, God will carry you in God's heart. Feel your body coming back to life—its bones, its flesh, its organs, its limbs, its heart.

Don't stay in exile anymore. That's not the place for you. God doesn't want you there. *Here* is your God. Speaking tenderly to you.

# 9

## Many a True Word

The film *Priest*[1] introduces us to Father Greg, a young and rather earnest Catholic priest, new to parish ministry. The movie centers on two issues that torture and dominate his life. The first is that he's gay. Finding no legitimate outlet for this emerging part of his identity, he begins a secret relationship with a man he meets in a bar. The second is that he hears the confession of a teenage girl called Lisa. He learns that she is regularly being intimately abused by her father. Later the father comes to confession too, and the priest is horrified to realize that this man bears scarcely any remorse for what he is doing. The seal of the confessional means Father Greg cannot communicate this information to anyone. But he struggles with that fact just as he wrestles with his own sexual identity. The power of his ability to pronounce or withhold forgiveness feels like nothing compared to his powerlessness to stop this terrible domestic tyranny. The two traumas of his life come to a crisis at much the same time. He faces the humiliation of being arrested for behaving improperly with another man in a public place. He has the book thrown at him by his bishop, and is forced to leave

---

1. Screenplay by Jimmy McGovern, directed by Antonia Bird (Burbank, CA: Miramax Home Entertainment, 1994), videocassette (VHS).

the parish. Meanwhile the truth of Lisa's domestic ordeal suddenly comes to light. In a harrowing scene, Lisa's mother emerges from an angry crowd, and, squaring up to Father Greg, with a tearful, bitter, and unforgiving gaze, says to him, "You knew." Father Greg has no idea what to say. Lisa's mother, now in disbelief and with her fury momentarily diverted from her husband and focused on her fragile and despised priest, says, vengefully, "You *knew*."

This is the church Jesus died for. A church with lots of rules designed to keep us just and make us holy. Sometimes those rules are such that, try as we might, we can't keep them. Other times those rules are ones the keeping of which opens us to bitterness, fury, and even hatred. The movie shows us both dimensions in the life of Father Greg. Either way, the church is exposed to public hatred and ridicule.

Public hatred and ridicule is the way the people of Jerusalem receive Jesus's crucifixion in the Gospel of Matthew. Everything around the cross happens in threes. There have been three predictions of the passion. Then Jesus makes three predictions of who will betray him—first Judas, then all the disciples, then Peter. Jesus prays three times in Gethsemane. Peter denies Jesus three times. After Jesus dies, three kinds of witnesses cluster around him: the soldiers, the women, and Joseph of Arimathea.

At the foot of the cross, there are three kinds of mockers. The first are the passersby, who say, "You who would destroy the temple and build it in three days, save yourself! If you are the Son of God, come down from the cross" (Matt. 27:40). Then there are the chief priests, along with the scribes and elders, who say, "He saved others; he cannot save himself. He is the King of Israel; let him come down from the cross now, and we will believe in him. He trusts in God; let God deliver him now, if he wants to; for he said, 'I am God's Son'" (Matt. 27:42–43). Finally there are the bandits who are crucified with him who taunt him in the same way. This threefold taunting at the climax of Jesus's ministry echoes the threefold temptation at the outset of his ministry. In case there's any doubt of the connection, we get the same phrase used on both occasions—"If you are the Son of God." Both the devil and the mockers goad Jesus with his apparent inactivity. Surely a real divine being would offer fireworks and spectacle, not silent resignation? Come on, Jesus, you can do better than this! How can you be the Messiah if you do nothing?

But the secret of the crucifixion scene is that there are many true words spoken in jest. Between them, this array of mockers gathered around Jesus succeeds in summarizing and affirming pretty much every truth the Gospel of Matthew seeks to communicate. Let's take them one by one.

The passersby say, "You who would destroy the temple and build it in three days." There are two ironies here. One is that this of course is exactly what Jesus is about to do—have his body destroyed and rebuilt in three days. The other is that the temple seemed the most indomitable feature of Israel's life. It had been destroyed once upon a time, and it had taken a hundred years to rebuild it. It had been severely damaged later and had taken two hundred years to restore the second time. By the time Matthew's Gospel was written, it had been destroyed a third and final time . . . but Jesus was very much alive. The mockers take for granted that the temple is permanent and Jesus is transitory. It turns out it's the other way round.

The passersby continue, "Save yourself and us." But Jesus has already said, "Those who want to save their life will lose it, and those who lose their life for my sake will find it" (Matt. 16:25). There's almost nothing the mockers can say that Jesus hasn't anticipated in his public ministry.

Both the passersby and the temple authorities say, "If you are the Son of God" and "he said, 'I am God's Son.'" But the ironic truth is, nowhere in the Gospel of Matthew does Jesus describe himself as the Son of God. The angel says it at his birth, the voice from the cloud says it at his transfiguration on the mountain, the centurion at the cross says it—but Jesus never says it. Somehow the mockers have intuited something Jesus has never said, and in trying to deride him they are in fact speaking a true word.

Then the passersby say, "Come down from the cross." But Jesus has already said, "If any want to become my followers, let them deny themselves and take up their cross and follow me" (Matt. 16:24). Once again, the mockers simply highlight the gospel Jesus has already proclaimed.

Of all the ironic statements at the foot of the cross, the most poignant are the words of the temple authorities, who say, "He saved others; he cannot save himself." This perfectly sums up the story that Matthew tells. It's a double irony because the authorities think the joke is on Jesus, and that they're identifying the irony that Jesus can't do for himself what he can do for others. But meanwhile what they *can't* see is that the joke is finally on them, because first of all they've been drawn into identifying that Jesus has *indeed* saved others, a major acknowledgment for them to make, and second that there's something unique about Jesus that makes both him and his suffering different from others. And that pretty much sums up the gospel. Jesus saves us but at terrible cost to himself.

When you look at your life, what do you see? Do you see a mockery of Jesus? In the movie, that's what Father Greg saw. He saw a bunch of well-intentioned rules, designed to guide people on the right path and restore them when they went astray. But he found he couldn't keep the rules designed to keep him on the path, and the rules designed to restore his parishioners when they strayed seemed to make him powerless when he most needed strength. Lisa's mother pointed her finger at him when he was down, with all the uninhibited hatred the mockers aimed at Jesus on the cross. "For a moment there I almost trusted you, I almost believed in you, you useless, pretentious, hypocritical creep."

Our lives are indeed a perpetual mockery of Jesus. Our work is a parody of the self-sacrificial, other-centered example of our Lord. Our relationships are a parody of the mutual-indwelling, abiding trust of the Trinity. Our discipleship walk is a parody of the disciplined fraternal correction and compassionate forbearance Jesus commends. Our mission is a parody of humble and constant presence among the hungry, the naked, the stranger, the sick, and the prisoner. Our congregational life is more like a squabble between self-righteous elder brothers than a welcome reception for prodigal sons. We are constantly at the foot of the cross, mocking the suffering Jesus.

But here's the irony. The more we mock, the truer Jesus becomes. The worse we fail, the greater grows our admiration and wonder at Jesus. The more pitiful our attempts to be faithful, the more necessary is our need for grace. The more we shout and scream at Jesus to come down from the cross, the more essential it is that he hangs there. The more we deride him and taunt him to save himself, the more we need him to save us. The more the church fails, the more we highlight the truth and urgent necessity of Jesus's person and message.

The climax of the gospel contains two great miracles. One is obvious, the one that God did—the miracle of resurrection. The other is subtler, and it comes right at this moment in Matthew's Gospel. It is the miracle of what Jesus *didn't* do. He didn't come down from the cross. He stayed there. He outlasted our hatred and cruelty and enmity. After everything humanity could throw at him, physically and verbally, he was still there. His endurance demonstrated the love that will never let us go. His perseverance showed that nothing can separate us from the love of God. From now on, forever, we can connect to God, not through our striving but through Jesus's suffering, not through our longing but through his lingering, not through our achieving but through his abiding.

It's not the Jesus we want. We want the Jesus who comes down from the cross, the Jesus who rights wrongs, ends pain, corrects injustice, sends the wicked away empty, sets the record straight, and makes all well with the world. We want answers. We want solutions. We want a technological Jesus who fixes the problems. And we want those problems fixed now. We want the Jesus that comes down from the cross. This Jesus will not come down from the cross. This Jesus bears all things, endures all things, and never ends. . . . This is not the God we want.

But it's the God we *need*. Oh how badly we need that God! Answers, explanations, solutions—they don't give us what we fundamentally need in the face of suffering and sin. What we need is love. What we need is a wondrous love through all eternity. Sure, what we *do* is show our inability to express that love. So we wash our hands like Pilate or run away like the disciples or lose patience like Judas or settle it with a sword like Peter. And so all the more what we *need* is a love that abides, that perseveres, that remains present to us, however bad things are, for however long it takes. What we *need* is a love that sticks around, a love that stays put, a love that hangs on. That's what the cross is. A love that hangs on.

I've presided over countless funerals in English working-class communities, and spent many hours trying to extract from mourners nuggets of wisdom and insight to give a personal touch to a funeral sermon. Of all those cameos, the most perennial is "He was always there for you." I've long pondered this ubiquitous phrase. Does it mean he was never out when you called? Does it mean simply you can't imagine life without her? I've come to the conclusion that it means what mattered was this man's presence, this woman's wordless permanence, their abiding touch. "She was always there for you." I used to mock this phrase as a banal cliché that had no purchase in any specific personal quality or characteristic. But I've come to understand that this invariable description of the deeply mourned, "He was always there for you," is none other than a description of the crucified God. We look at Jesus on the cross, and we say to one another, "He's always there . . . for *you*."

The end of the film *Priest* contains the most moving scene I've ever witnessed in the cinema. Father Greg returns to the parish after his time of humiliation and exile. The anger and hatred still smolders in the neighborhood and the parish. Lisa's mother's incandescent words, "*You knew*," are still ringing in his and our ears. Lisa hasn't been seen in the church since the truth about her household came to light. The senior priest, Father Matthew, implores the congregation to receive Father Greg back as their father in God. When it comes to receiving Communion there are two stations for taking the bread, one from Father Matthew, the other from Father Greg. Every single worshiper at the service lines up to receive from Father Matthew. Father Greg stands alone, the body of Christ in his hands, totally shunned and visibly humiliated by the whole congregation. Seconds tick by and his isolation is crucifying. Somehow he has the courage and defiance to continue to stand alone—to hang in there. And then slowly but purposefully one solitary figure shuffles forward and stands before him to receive Communion. It's Lisa.

Their eyes meet as she receives the Communion bread. Her eyes say, "I know that you knew about my dad. But I know that you couldn't do anything about it. I understand your present powerlessness. I know it's because you believe in a greater power. You show me that by your courage in being present here right now. You're being crucified, but you're showing us a love that will not let us go."

That's the irony of the cross. If Jesus had saved himself, he couldn't have saved us. His powerlessness shows us the endurance of God. Jesus hangs on the cross to show us the love that hangs on. Hang on to that love. It will never let you go.

# 10

# I Have No Need of You

Some years ago I had a clergy colleague who had an unusual way of finishing the Sunday service. He used to bow down to the congregation. He would say, "Some clergy bow before the altar and some bow before the cross. But I'm told that these people are the body of Christ, so I bow before them."

In 1 Corinthians 12 Paul tells us that each part of the church, each member of the church, is like an eye or an ear or a hand. The foot can't say to the hand, "I don't need you," nor can the eye say to the rest, "I'm the whole body." And Paul underlines that the weaker members of the body are vital to the health and welfare of the body. What does Paul mean?

Almost forty years ago Richard Adams published the book *Watership Down*, a novel about rabbits.[1] It tells the story of a dozen rabbits who search for a warren to call home. The novel is given a sharp edge by the way each of the communities the rabbits encounters has its own political system. The warren at the beginning of the novel is like a traditional, hierarchical society. The rabbits run away from that warren because they correctly anticipate that it's about to be destroyed by humans. A second warren the rabbits meet

1. Richard Adams, *Watership Down* (1972; repr., New York: Scribner, 2005).

is run on a totalitarian model. There is one general who keeps all the other rabbits in a state of fear under a military regime. A third community of rabbits seems to resemble a modern decadent society. The rabbits there are somewhat inebriated. Food is plentiful and the living is easy. But the rabbits have lost the ability to find their own food and, more seriously, the ability to tell the truth. They can't bring themselves to acknowledge that they're under the spell of a farmer who feeds them but also snares and kills them one by one. The fourth warren is the one the rabbits establish for themselves on the hill called Watership Down.

The rabbits discover a great many things through their travels and adventures. But perhaps the most important thing they discover is that they need each other. One of the rabbits is big and strong, another is quick thinking and imaginative, a third is speedy, a fourth is fiercely loyal, a fifth is a good storyteller. Perhaps the key rabbit is the smallest and clumsiest, but who has a sixth sense that anticipates danger—like the destruction of the original warren. What makes this group of rabbits so significant is that they find ways of using the gifts of every member of the party so that they are never short of wisdom and intelligence about what to do next, or courage and strength to do what is needed. In other words, the group of rabbits lives and moves and thinks as one body rather than as a dozen separate bodies. There can't be such a thing as an idea or a development that is good for one of the rabbits but not good for the whole body.

To be a part of a group like that group of rabbits can be a wonderful experience. One of the fascinations of team sports is that a group will only succeed if it has a mixture of speed, size, strength, hand-eye coordination, determination, courage, and imagination, and the breakthrough comes when the members of the team realize it's not about any one of them being the star but about each of them realizing how much they need each other. The same is broadly true for actors putting on a play, musicians participating in an orchestra, and singers joining a choir. The soprano doesn't say to the alto halfway through Handel's *Messiah*, "I have no need of you."

So being one body is a familiar human experience. But I think this group of rabbits offers us a particular series of lessons about what it might mean to be the church. I'm going to suggest three such lessons.

First, we can never say we've "made it." The rabbits in the story are like Christians making their way through life—they are longing to get to the point where they can say, "Phew—that's it. We've made it." Well, there is no such point. Teenagers long to leave home, undergraduates long to get a degree, graduates long for the PhD or the first professional paycheck, faculty for tenure, parents for the first child, homeowners to pay off the mortgage, pension savers for a healthy retirement. And churches are the same. They long to pay for the new building, open the outreach program, finally get a decent preacher, and sort out the music. But the moment never comes. And the story of the rabbits shows us why it shouldn't. Because when the dozen refugees meet the easy-living rabbits who live the good life, they can see quite quickly that those inebriated rabbits have lost what it takes to be a community, to tell the truth, and ultimately to survive.

The church will always remain a pilgrim people. Whenever you meet a bunch of Christians who feel they've "made it," whether in strength of numbers, firmness of doctrine, righteousness of attitude, or purity of life, you can anticipate that pretty soon they'll be in trouble. Israel was formed on the way from Egypt to the Promised Land. The disciples were formed on the way from Galilee to Jerusalem. The church becomes one body as it is bound together on its common journey. It's always a work in progress.

Seeing ourselves as a pilgrim people should help us avoid the twin temptations of identifying too strongly with our culture or sealing ourselves off from it. We can't live in this culture as if it were our permanent home. But the fact that we have promises to keep elsewhere doesn't make this culture inherently bad. On the contrary, the gifts God gives us for the journey don't just come from one another: they often come from strangers. The rabbits in the story receive vital help and intervention from a bird who can see things they can't and from a young girl at a farm who saves one of the rabbits from her cat. The pilgrim church likewise must be open to receiving surprising gifts from those it might regard as strangers, like the bird, or even, like the farm girl, enemies.

Second, the diversity of the church is a strength, not a weakness. The group of rabbits survives only because it has rabbits with different gifts, different strengths, different visions for what they are doing and where they are going. Paul says there are varieties of gifts but the same Spirit, varieties of ways of serving God but the same Lord. Paul may have seen it that way, but it's hardly a fashionable view among Christians today. Today we say to one another, "If you're a different color, you need to be in a different church. If you're a different gender, at least if you want to be in ministry, you need to be in a different church. If you're a different sexual orientation, you need to be in a different church. If you play music according to the custom of a different century, you need to be in a different church. If you have a rival understanding of liturgy, or the Bible, or baptism, or most ironically, spiritual gifts, you need to be in a different church."

I expect you know the story of the man who arrived on a desert island to be greeted by the sole occupant of the island. He noticed there were two buildings on the island, and asked what the first one was. "That's my church," said the sole occupant. "And the other building, over there?" asked the visitor. "That's the church I wouldn't be caught dead in." And that's the tragedy and the scandal of the contemporary church. If you asked most American Christians, especially progressive Christians, who the enemy is, they'd most likely say the enemy is other Christians. And the internet makes it much worse, because there judgmental Christians using the shield of anonymity pass on hearsay and half-truth about apparently ghastly things alleged to be happening in formerly respectable churches—a practice that used to be called malicious and self-righteous gossip but is now called blogging.

There's another well-known story about a monastery where the monks were constantly at each other's throats, bickering and cursing at one another. One night a mysterious visitor knocked at the monastery door and made a brief but solemn announcement. "One of you is Jesus Christ." The atmosphere in the monastery changed overnight. Suddenly each monk treated every other monk with awe and wonder, not sure which one was Jesus but knowing Jesus was among them. They had learned what it means to be the church—to treat one another as we would treat Jesus, to expect from one another all that Jesus brings, to cherish one another as we cherish Jesus. And if we do this for individuals, why can we not do so for denominations, for traditions, for styles of worship, and for understandings of humanity different from our own?

Take one example. The Bible is made up of sixty-six books. Each is different—some are very different from one another—and one or two even seem to contradict one another. And yet almost all Christians regard the whole Bible as God's gift to the church to reveal God's character and disclose God's purpose. If we take it for granted that these sixty-six books work together to reveal God, why can't we take it for granted that these thousands of denominations can also be places where God is made known? And if we can't do without any of the sixty-six books and still have all we need to know about God, how can we do without any of these other ways of being Christian? We need each other. We need each other to know God. We cannot say to one another, "I have no need of you."

The third thing we learn from the rabbits of *Watership Down* is that being one body isn't just a matter of ignoring differences, allowing tolerance to break out, and dimming the lights to a point where all the rabbits are gray. What saves the rabbits at crucial moments in the narrative is their willingness and commitment to listen to one another, to hear each other out when they have stories, worries, misgivings, or hopes. Out of these curious memories and visions come the gifts that make the group of rabbits so resilient and so adaptable. Being part of a church that is one body means taking the time to listen to one another's stories—stories of why one group felt it needed to break away and how another group came to be pushed out, stories of how one group came to regard as central an issue most others regard as peripheral, stories of how so many have felt that unity and truth were separable and that they could somehow make it on their own.

Being one body doesn't just mean that the eye can't say to the hand, "I have no need of you." It means that if the eye is in pain, the whole body is in pain, and the hand does whatever it can to make things better. Paul's picture isn't about bland tolerance. It's about shared direction, shared wisdom, and shared pain. Being one body is probably a lot more painful than going our separate ways. We spend a lot of our time searching around for vital things we have to do that make listening to one another's stories seem like a waste of time. But Paul says to us, "Your mission is to be one body. Your message is that Christ has made you one body. There isn't anything more important for you to rush off to."

So these are the three lessons of 1 Corinthians 12, as mirrored by the rabbits of *Watership Down*. First, we can never say we've made it. All church life is provisional. We are a pilgrim people. Second, diversity is a gift and a strength, not a weakness or a sin of unfaithfulness. Third, unity is something you have to work at, and that work is not a distraction but is at the heart of the gospel.

Of course there's one thing we don't learn from the rabbits, and that's that we're talking not about any old body but about the body of Christ. Rabbits can show us what it means to live as a body, but baptism is what shows us what it means to be the body of Christ. If we weren't interested in the unity of the church, we shouldn't have been baptized. Telling another Christian, "I have no need of you" is really telling Jesus, "I have no need of you."

No Christian is in a position to say to any other, "I have no need of you." Every Christian needs to listen to the stories of those who see things differently, have been pushed out or felt they had to leave. Church means calling together Christians of all kinds, in all ways, across all barriers, and bringing them face-to-face, and holding them there in the presence of God, until they say to one another, "I need you."

# PART 3

# be not afraid of power

Along with all my seminary class, I left seminary confused about power. All of us knew power was a bad thing. All of us knew that "among the Gentiles those whom they recognize as their rulers lord it over them, and their great ones are tyrants over them" (Mark 10:42). All of us knew that it was not to be so among us, and all of us knew the words "Whoever wishes to become great among you must be your servant, and whoever wishes to be first among you must be slave of all" (Mark 10:44). We were also just beginning to discover that since most of us were white Western males, who had for countless generations regarded ourselves as the center of the universe, we were crossing a threshold from an era where we were the standard of virtue to one where we were the measure of vice. And we were being ordained into a church that was becoming obsessed with its loss of numbers, money, and social influence, and that was forgetting that numbers, money, and social influence obscure the power of the gospel at least as often as they reveal it.

The result was that we were a generation who had no idea of our own power. We had no vocabulary for it, no social legitimacy for it, no theology for it, no encouragement for it. And so those of us who fell into despair, anger, depression, or displaced desperation for security or love did so more than anything else out of a sense of powerlessness. If we did damage to our church members or our tradition, it was less through reckless use of intoxicating power than through ignorance of the power we had. I consider myself lucky to have recently had the experience of living in the American South, a culture where the churches, considered together, have all the things the Church of England thinks it needs—numbers, money, and social influence. But it turns out that the kingdom of God is no closer. Living in this rather different culture and seeing the same questions from more than one point of view has helped me better understand and appreciate where the power of the gospel truly lies, and why it's nothing to fear.

# 11

# By What Authority?

When people like to feel that they're living in interesting times, they often refer to a sense of crisis. It might be the financial markets, global warming, or international terrorism. Once it was the collapse of communism and the threat of global nuclear annihilation. But there's one crisis that's been going on for a good couple of hundred years or more: a crisis of authority.

When I was in eighth grade, my class had a particularly ineffectual teacher. Being cruel in the way that only eighth graders know how, every time he turned his back to write on the chalkboard, we all used to edge our desks forward a few inches. Eventually the front row was only a couple of feet from him. The poor man was helpless. We had no respect for him. For the first time I began to reflect on where authority comes from.

This is the question Jesus is asked in Matthew 21: "By what authority are you doing these things, and who gave you this authority?" (Matt. 21:23). Throughout his Gospel, Matthew portrays an alliance against Jesus, an alliance whose membership is constantly changing. At the beginning, in the wise men story, Herod calls the chief priests and scribes (Matt. 2); early on, the conspiracy is conducted by the Pharisees alone (Matt. 12); later, Jesus is approached

69

by Pharisees and scribes (Matt. 15); when Jesus predicts his arrest, he identifies his accusers as the elders along with the chief priests and scribes (Matt. 16); early in chapter 21 it's the chief priests and scribes again, and later it's the chief priests and the elders. Toward the end of chapter 21, in the conversation with Jesus in the temple, it's the chief priests and the Pharisees.

A casual reading might suggest these groups are interchangeable. But that would miss the point. The point is that these groups represent the conventional forms of established authority in ancient society. The chief priests represent the authority of birth, the scribes represent the authority of education, the Pharisees represent the authority of strict religious observance, and the elders represent the authority of wealth and social connections. They come to Jesus and ask him, "By what authority do you waltz into the temple and overturn the tables and perform healings and make all this mayhem? Just who exactly do you think you are?" They're assuming they're asking a question to which they themselves embody all the available answers.

The question of authority goes right to the heart of the gospel and right to the heart of society. In the Middle Ages, while money and social connections could give you power, there was no chronic crisis of authority in the sense that we have today. Since God was the unquestioned source of authority, God's representatives on earth, while they might not have the greatest executive power, nonetheless had the highest authority. Meanwhile the Greeks and Romans were generally assumed to be the only people who'd ever got civilization right; and so wisdom and institutions directly derived from the classical era were a source of authority complementary to the church.

The Reformation shook this consensus over authority because it shifted authority from institutions and individuals to a particular book, the Bible. Proclaiming the authority of Scripture was supposed to unite everyone around a fixed and unchanging, even infallible, point of authority. In fact, it had the opposite result. Once growing literacy and the printing press meant that everyone got to read it for themselves, it turned out they each came to drastically different conclusions about what it meant. Authority came to lie not so much in the book but in those regarded as the interpreters of the book. And so the Protestant churches ended up reinventing their own versions of

70

the old authority structures they'd worked so hard to abolish. The trouble was that now there were dozens of rival authority structures.

The old consensus over authority had gone. The period known as the Enlightenment, beginning around 1700, finished the job. The Enlightenment said authority lay not in ancient documents, venerable institutions, or inspired leaders but in the heart of each individual. So the American and French Revolutions invested authority not in God, in the church, or in the Bible but in the people. They introduced a new religion, which said that the voice of the people was the voice of God.

And that's the moment when the age-old *question* of authority turns into the very contemporary *crisis* of authority. Because now we don't just have rival squabbling authorities, we suddenly have something more *important* than authority, something called freedom. Freedom is what I feel is right for me. Authority is what others believe is best for everyone. Freedom is the voice that comes from within me. Authority is the voice that comes from within others. But I only really trust the voice that comes from within me. When *your* authority seems to limit *my* freedom, I describe you as authoritarian. No one wants to be called authoritarian. And that shows that most people in a culture like ours value freedom more than they value authority. We have no final arbiter between our desires and the good of others, which is why we have a crisis of authority.

So the crisis of authority is over two hundred years old. If Jesus were hanging out with the disciples in the public square today, the people who would question his authority wouldn't be Pharisees, elders, chief priests, and scribes, they'd be more familiar faces. They'd be the shadowy multinational corporate executives, who stand to gain by shoehorning their candidate into the White House; they'd be the leading scientific minds of our universities, used to being the authorities on undisputed facts; they'd be the psychological experts, used to dealing with self-proclaimed messiahs with delusions of grandeur; they'd be media moguls, used to shaping public opinion by claiming simply to reflect it.

What these figures have in common is that they represent the two kinds of authority that emerged from this historical legacy and carry weight today. One is the authority of *force* and the other's the authority of *function*.

71

The first one is really about power. Let's go back to my exasperated eighth-grade teacher for a moment. He'd clearly lost the moral power of persuasion. As our desks slid slowly toward him like an advancing army, he used to plead, with forced cheerfulness, "Okay now, you've had your fun, let's get down to work." But to his horror, my teacher found the desks just kept advancing. The real question is, as every parent, teacher, police officer, or failing despot knows deep inside, when the moral power of persuasion fails, can one turn to the physical power of coercion? Since corporal punishment went out of fashion, the tension in the classroom is always to see whether the teacher can maintain authority without any resort to physical intimidation. In the days when all political power was regarded as being held in trust from God, there seemed to be an authority that went beyond physical force. Today it's not so easy.

The second kind of authority is less about naked power and more about effective procedure. When someone lists a whole load of degrees after their name or offers you a résumé with a fistful of senior appointments, they're not using coercion, they're just telling you that they are people who know how to run things, how to make things work, how to get the best out of other people, when to make a change, and when to wait and see. When a company tells you it's proudly been making an unwanted-facial-hair remover since 1957 or a meeting chair says, "Let's now turn to item four on the agenda," the kind of authority involved is one that says, "This is the best way to do things, this is really in everyone's interests, trust me, I've done this before, it'll work."

So these are the two kinds of authority most widely recognized today. On the one hand you have a *functional* authority, which rests on a proven record of making things work. On the other hand you have simple *force*, which has to be respected but only really comes into play when it's lost the argument.

What kind of authority does Jesus have? Well, we could say God's authority is fundamentally about *coercion*. We could say God made heaven and earth and spins the universe on his finger like a Frisbee. God gives us life, God determines the moment of our death, and God chooses if we qualify for eternal life. That's power. And if we take that line, Jesus's authority is rooted in his power: just look at the miracles. Or alternatively we could say Christianity basically *works*. It encourages people to keep their promises, pay back their debts, stick with their families, honor their parents, and keep damaging feuds to a minimum. It's quite compatible with democracy, capitalism, and the free market.

When people get angry with Christianity and/or the church, it's usually because they reject its authority on one of these two grounds. Either they say Christianity doesn't work, or they say Christianity is no more than a mask for coercion. When people say Christianity doesn't work, they refer to the failure of its descriptive power in accounting for suffering, other faiths, or the evidence of scientific inquiry; or they refer to the failure of its prescriptive power in genuinely making better people, healing communities, or bringing peace to the world. When people say Christianity is no more than a mask for coercion, they tend to imply the Christian story is little more than a veneer of respectability painted over human ambition and the desire for control.

But maybe there's another kind of authority. Maybe there's a kind of authority that goes beyond the antagonism of naked power and the cynicism of established procedure. Maybe there's an authority that sometimes appears weak and even unpopular but will abide whether people follow it or not, an authority that has no need of manipulation because it has no interest in deceiving people, an authority that doesn't have to be articulate and stylish because it's just as well represented by the clumsy and the stumbling, an authority whose simplicity is transparency, whose identity is generosity, whose witness is its beauty. Maybe there's a kind of authority called the authority of truth. Jesus says, "Believe in me not because you have to, not because it works, but because in me you've come face-to-face with truth." Jesus challenges his accusers to answer one question: "Did the baptism of John come from heaven, or was it of human origin?" (Matt. 21:25). And they're forced to reply that they don't know, because either answer will get them into trouble. "You never really knew who John the Baptist was," Jesus tells his accusers. "But you knew that in him you'd met the truth. Smelly and angry as he was, much as you could have done without the locusts and the camel's hair shirt, now that he's dead you realize he was the real deal."

Throughout the last two centuries there have always been Christians trying to get Jesus's authority onto firmer ground, looking for knockdown evidence, trying to show God's power by proving the miracles or trying to demonstrate Christianity's plausibility by grounding it on more fashionable forms of human knowledge. But these efforts will never come off. They rest on a mistaken notion of authority. Jesus comes to us as the truth, no more and no less. We can't begin somewhere else and somehow reason our way to Jesus. However we come to meet Jesus, when we come face-to-face with him, when he sees through us with his fully knowing yet utterly loving gaze, all other truth, all other knowledge, all other relationships, all other authority, has to step back into line behind this truth, this knowledge, this relationship, this authority. Whenever we ground the authority of Jesus on some other authority, we make that other authority more fundamental than Jesus. There's *nothing* more fundamental than Jesus, and what God is doing in Jesus. That's what Jesus's authority means.

And this is the crucial point. If we rest in the authority of truth, the truth that meets us in Jesus makes us let go of the authority of effectiveness and coercion. Jesus has a way of doing things that challenges the time-honored procedures of worldly authority. Jesus has a power that runs counter to worldly power. If we've come to Jesus looking for an authority to underwrite the authority of coercion and effectiveness, we've come to the wrong place. The authority of Jesus doesn't explicitly make things happen, doesn't always ensure things run smoothly, but it does hold a distinct advantage over other authorities by being true. Coercion and effectiveness are what you fall back on once you stop believing Christianity is fundamentally true.

The people I look up to are the people who have the authority of truth. I think of a friend who never shouts, never exaggerates, never ingratiates, but simply lets her quiet yes be yes and her quiet no be no. I think of a politician who, when he realized he was wrong, said, "When I realize I'm wrong, I change my mind—what do you do?" I think of a colleague who was deeply hurt by a friend and yet through his tears said, "I'm not going to let the bitterness of this injury determine the shape of my future life." I think of a woman who simply listens to people for as long as it takes for them to find the sense in their troubled lives. I think of an executive who stayed in his job under terrible pressure because he firmly believed he'd done nothing wrong and to resign would mean leaving the company in the hands of his unscrupulous employers. I think of a teacher who kept going in a failing school because he believed whatever it was these children needed, education had to be a big part of it. These are the people I look up to. They have no handle on coercion. They wouldn't pass any conventional test of effectiveness. But they have something more precious. They have the authority of truth. These people are Jesus for me.

What authority do you have? Are you admired, perhaps even feared, because you are powerful? Are you respected, perhaps even imitated, because you are effective and get the job done? Or do you have another kind of authority, which isn't about being in charge and isn't about getting things done, but rests on a confidence that God is fundamentally in charge and that in Jesus, God has done what fundamentally needs to be done? When others see you, do they see that authority? It may be quiet, it may be understated, it may be clumsy, it may be inarticulate, it may be stumbling, it may be a little unsure of itself. But in the end, it's the only authority that matters. It'll be around long after coercion and effectiveness have faded away. It's Jesus's authority, and it's called the authority of truth.

# 12

## But It Shall Not
## Be So with You

When I was growing up in England, America was a faraway place made up of four states—California, Texas, Florida, and New York. I knew the word *Watergate* and I knew it meant something very sad that my American godfather didn't want to talk about. I knew the word *Vietnam* and I knew he didn't much want to talk about that either. I remember that a man from Georgia with a very big smile was elected president. No one was sure if that might mean some kind of new start for America, although I got the impression it was certainly a big day for peanut farmers. But one very vivid memory is of President Carter late in his presidency going for a jog with his aides and being overcome by some kind of heat exhaustion. From three thousand miles away it felt like America could cope with crooked politicians and a war that ran into the sand but it couldn't somehow deal with a weak leader.

Very little has changed in thirty years. We can't agree on what's wrong and we aren't at all sure where we should be going, but we all know we need a great leader. If there's one thing every high school senior knows that they must put on their application to college, it's their astonishing record of leadership. "While still in the womb I spearheaded the movement for my twin and me to enter the birth canal." "While still in nursery I organized the toddlers to campaign for recyclable diapers." "While in first grade I represented my class at the school board showdown on whether to move to 2 percent milk at snack time." "When I was in fourth grade I went on a Girl Scout expedition to the planet Jupiter, and devised a system by which children could share oxygen on the return journey, to save on baggage weight." "When I was in eighth grade I scythed deep into the Amazonian jungle, and found a previously unknown tribe. I learned their language, taught them how to play golf, and helped them find a sustainable water supply."

If colleges believe their own publicity, they are factories for manufacturing leaders. They don't ask too much about what other institutions do, but presumably someone out there must be manufacturing followers: otherwise things are going to get a little unbalanced. The trouble is, while we assume leadership is the answer to everything, we are extremely skeptical about leaders themselves. We're always alert to ways in which leaders may simply be using the people or organization they lead to gain some nefarious benefit for themselves—a bloated salary, some kind of gravy-train vacation perk, an opportunity to foster some possibly illegal business venture, or (and now I speak in hushed tones) the most highly prized commodities in corporate life: an office with windows and a convenient parking space. Colleges train young people to be extremely ambitious but point them toward roles in which they will inevitably attract suspicion, cynicism, and outright hostility.

Jesus is well aware of the problem. His close friends James and John have more than half an eye on the perks and the public acclaim. They've already selected their heavenly parking spots and tenured offices. Jesus tells them they've lost the plot. "Whoever wishes to become great among you must be your *servant*, and whoever wishes to be first among you must be *slave of all*" (Mark 10:43–44, emphasis added). So where does that put our obsession with leadership? How can you be a ruler and a slave at the same time? That's the question I want to examine here.

It's worth setting out in a bit of detail what being a leader involves, to get a sense of what Jesus is challenging and what he's affirming.

77

To be a leader is to be expected to do four things. Imagine four points of a square.

At the top left of the square is the role of spokesperson. This is someone who is good with words, a figurehead who can talk with people outside an organization to explain what it is and inspire interest and trust in what it does. At the same time, they use words to motivate and instruct those within the organization about where they are going and how they may best get there. When outsiders think of the organization it's the spokesperson who gives it an immediately identifiable human face. When you think of civil rights you think of Martin Luther King Jr., when you think of charitable work among the poor you think of Mother Teresa, and when you think of the antiapartheid struggle you think of Nelson Mandela, because these are the people who give outsiders a human face through which to comprehend complex and diverse movements.

Then at the top right of the square is the role of the chair. The chair is the one who ensures that rules are kept, that deadlines are met, that obligations are carried out, that the organization fulfills its mission, that everyone does their job properly, that each person gets paid, that the right people are hired, and that the noisy don't dominate and the shy don't evaporate. If the spokesperson is about inspiration, the chair is about permanence and trust. The person in charge often carries responsibility for a lot of people's welfare and institutional capital, let alone the money side of things, and you want a chair to be a safe and competent pair of hands. In short, the chair is the grown-up. However much you may admire someone, if they're always losing checks or forgetting appointments or constantly late for meetings, they may be a charismatic presence, but you're not going to want them in charge of your organization for long.

At the bottom left of the square is the role of facilitator. If the chair leads from the front, the facilitator leads from the back. The facilitator is like the athletics coach, constantly going round the team to have a quiet word with each one, working out how to get the best out of them all and how to get the right combinations to release the energy in the group. This is the person who remembers everyone's birthday and organizes terrific leaving parties, who turns conflict into an opportunity for growth, treats crisis as an invitation to creativity, and sees no mistakes or failures, only bonding moments and learning experiences. If the chair makes you feel everything's under control, the facilitator makes you feel you're having a good time. You didn't realize you were dying to dress up as dinosaurs and have a staff night out at the all-you-can-eat ice cream parlor, but afterward you all said it was great to let your hair down and we should do it again.

And at the bottom right of the square is the role of the epitome. This is the person who represents all that's good about an organization. They try the hardest, they wake at night thinking about crucial details, and their actions perfectly embody everything the institution stands for. If the spokesperson is all about words, then the epitome is all about deeds. They may not be fantastically articulate, but when you prick them, they bleed with the lifeblood of the organization they serve. They're loyal, dogged, unwavering, and faithful. They're the captain who goes down with the ship. If they break with or fall short of the organization's high standards it feels catastrophic, because they somehow crystallize the institution's moral credibility. When people ask the leader, "How much are you paid?" or, "Where do your children go to school?" or, "What kind of car do you drive?" they may just be being nosy, but they may well be asking, "Just what exactly does this institution really stand for?" People sense that the leader's personal values should epitomize the perceived high values of the institution.

We expect our leaders to be outstanding in all of these roles. Of course this is a fantasy. No one is outstanding in all these roles. Wise leaders know where they are weak and harness the gifts and qualities of others to compensate for their own shortcomings. In fact it's often bad for an organization to have a supercompetent leader, because nothing grows in the shade of a great tree, and when the leader leaves or dies the grief can be paralyzing. That's the story of the demise of a thousand family businesses, when the great founder-patriarch dies having never given his children a chance to run things without his suffocating micromanagement.

All four dimensions of leadership have their distortions and temptations. The spokesperson may be a dilettante who just loves the flattery and attention of being in the public eye. The chair may be greedy in the sense of being in control of other people's lives and be inclined to take advantage of the perks and the privileges of power.

The facilitator may be seeking a perpetual high of life as a nonstop party and be overcompensating for shortcomings in their own family structure or close relationships. The epitome may be so wrapped up in the organization that they come to feel it's an extension of their own personality or family and may refuse to retire or be obstructive of change.

But Jesus is concerned about tyranny and making a show of leadership. He says, "You know that among the Gentiles those whom they recognize as their rulers lord it over them, and their great ones are tyrants over them" (Mark 10:42). He's putting the spotlight on leaders who are *using* their organizations or kingdoms for some purpose beyond the institution itself, usually personal aggrandizement or gratification. It seems this is the crucial point. The leader that Jesus applauds *has no ambition or goal beyond the organization they are leading*—it's not a source of wealth or vehicle for power or a platform for acclaim. It's an end in itself. That's why he uses the language of slavery. To us the word *slave* is profoundly jarring, even abhorrent—not just in the history of the American South but also in contemporary crimes such as human trafficking and sexual exploitation. Jesus isn't condoning any of these things. He wants us to imagine choosing to have no other outlet for our energies than to see others flourish. The kind of slavery Jesus means isn't a condition imposed on you by a tyrant. It's an attitude you *yourself* choose as a form of discipleship, as a way of saying, "I have no goal in life beyond bringing out the best in others." Jesus doesn't force us to be his slaves. He sets us free to choose to be slaves of all.

Some years ago I was closely involved in a large-scale, community-led economic redevelopment program. I poured a great number of hours into the process of shaping a plan, gaining funding, establishing a company, and trying to bring more jobs, better education, and better health to the neighborhood. Four or five years into the process, I found myself staying late after an evening meeting, having a disagreement with one of the most prominent neighborhood leaders. I was worn out and frustrated, and I said to her, "Why do you think I'm *involved* in this process? Why do you think I've been involved all *along*?" She said, without blinking, "I assume it's for the sake of your career." I was stunned. I didn't know whether to laugh or cry. I thought, "I live here; I don't live anywhere else. I've put a mountain of hours into this program. What do I have to do to show you I care about this place? And if you think this is the kind of neighborhood where career-hungry clergy spend their thirties, I've got news for you." But I didn't say it.

It hurt so much I still remember it several years later. But the trouble is, in an important way she was right. Not about the career, I hope. But she was really saying, "You'll never be the right leader for this community because your identity isn't sufficiently tied up in it." An epitome is someone who has no real aspirations beyond the organization. A facilitator is someone who has no joy in life beyond making everyone in the institution flourish. She was saying she didn't see those things in me. Sure, I could be a spokesperson between the high-ups in city hall and the local leaders, between the suits and the streets. And sure, I could chair meetings and keep us within the rules. But I was always going to be seeking my identity beyond and outside. She put her finger on that, while I refused to see it.

Jesus is saying that to be a leader like him, you need to share some characteristics with a slave. A slave has no identity that isn't wrapped up in their owner. A slave has no ability to flourish that isn't about the flourishing of others. These are the characteristics of what I've been calling the epitome and the facilitator. Is Jesus saying Christian leadership doesn't require the gifts of the chair and the spokesperson? No, I don't think so. Not all spokespersons and chairs tyrannize and lord it over people. The point is that *these are the areas where the most temptation lies.* And the best way to avoid the temptations latent in every leadership position is to be absolutely certain that you're aiming to be an epitome and a facilitator. Those are roles in which it's very hard to accumulate benefit for yourself that the organization never receives. These are inherently servant roles, where it's impossible for you to gain unless everyone else gains at the same time. Yes, absolutely be a spokesperson and a chair: these roles are integral to leadership, and no organization can run without them. But do so in a way that enables you always to remain an epitome who embodies what the organization is all about and a facilitator who brings out the best in everyone else. Concentrating on those roles is the best way, maybe the only way, to avoid the pitfalls of leadership.

And that means this isn't just a conversation about chief executives in leather-seated limousines. Not everyone gets to be the chair,

81

and not everyone is a good fit to be the visible spokesperson. But everyone can be the epitome of the organization they believe in, and everyone can spend their life bringing out the best in those around them. Jesus's final remarks identify himself—but they also challenge us. "The Son of Man came not to be served but to serve, and to *give his life* a ransom for many" (Mark 10:45, emphasis added). We all have to die sooner or later. Jesus tells us what he's going to die for. He's going to die because he epitomizes the kingdom he proclaims, and he's going to die to set people free. That's it. Just those two desires. He calls himself a slave because he has no desire beyond those two desires, no notion of personal benefit beyond the salvation of the world.

Do you have no desire beyond those two desires? Is that what *you* are going to die for? If so, you're what Jesus calls a leader. You're just the kind of leader Jesus wants.

# 13

# Giving with Your Head, Your Hand, and Your Heart

Many years ago I took a thirty-seven-hour train ride from Senegal to Mali. Mali is the poorest country in West Africa, and one of the poorest in the world. I recall walking around the streets of the capital, Bamako. My first reaction was, "Wow, it's hot." (This was before I'd ever spent a summer in North Carolina.) But then I felt completely confused. Should I give to the beggars?

I'd grown up with an elaborate protection system for my conscience. If I met a beggar at home in England I could rely on understanding the welfare system and then go into a conversation in my head about how best to give food and whether cash would be counterproductive if it was bound to be spent on drugs. As for poverty overseas—that was what aid agencies and government programs were for. I was aware of mutterings and cynicism about whether the money really got through to the people in need, but there wasn't a whole lot I could do about that.

But now there was. I found myself face-to-face with the poorest people in one of the poorest places in the world. And suddenly I was desperately scratching around for a hundred new reasons why

I shouldn't give them anything. "They're probably controlled by pimps. They wouldn't use the money wisely. If I give to one I'll be besieged by others." My self-protecting logic went into overdrive. "It's probably best to give to the agencies after all," I decided, and dove into the covered market.

I wonder how you react when you're asked for money. I wonder if you go into the same convulsions of panic, guilt, and self-justifying logic that I went through that hot dusty day in Bamako. I want to think about how our giving can move from paralysis to joy, from secrecy to transparency, from private embarrassment to shared pleasure.

In 1 Corinthians 16 and again in 2 Corinthians 8, Paul asks the Christians in Corinth to support the poor in Jerusalem. It's not clear whether the poor in Jerusalem means the struggling mother church in Jerusalem or the poor whom the church in Jerusalem is trying to serve. I'm going to assume it's both. I want to suggest today that giving is always about assisting the poor, building up the church, and deepening our own discipleship. In 2 Corinthians, Paul uses three kinds of arguments to persuade the Corinthians.

He starts by appealing to their *pride*. He tries to get them into a competition to give more than the Macedonians. First he points out that the Macedonians' abundant joy overflowed into a "wealth of generosity" even in spite of their "extreme poverty" (2 Cor. 8:2). Next he refers to giving as a "privilege," and then he slyly tells the Corinthians, "Now as you excel in everything—in faith, in speech, in knowledge, in utmost eagerness, and in our love for you—so we want you to excel also in this generous undertaking" (2 Cor. 8:7). He calls upon their sense of prudent financial management, to complete a commitment they initiated a year earlier, and only to give a realistic sum: "It is appropriate for you who began last year not only to do something but even to desire to do something—now finish doing it, so that your eagerness may be matched by completing it according to your means" (2 Cor. 8:10–11).

Next he holds up a mirror to their *faith* and *holiness*. He reminds them, "For you know the generous act of our Lord Jesus Christ, that though he was rich, yet for your sakes he became poor, so that by his poverty you might become rich" (2 Cor. 8:9). Almost goading the Corinthians, Paul implies, "Why wouldn't you want to be like that?"

Finally Paul subtly nudges their *self-interest*. Bring your present abundance to *their* need, he says, and they might be around to bring their future abundance to *your* need, should you find yourselves hard up one day (2 Cor. 8:13–15).

Think about it. Pride, faith, self-interest. It's an ambiguous list of reasons for giving money. When I left college at the age of twenty-two, I sensed a call to be ordained and I wanted to live with the poor, so I set about finding out if it was possible to do both at the same time. I moved to the poorest part of the poorest city in England. But deep down I knew this wasn't entirely for noble reasons. I knew whatever love and faithfulness I had was mixed up with anger and pride. I had all sorts of heart-searchings about what I was doing and why I was doing it. I knew T. S. Eliot's line that the worst treason was to do the right thing for the wrong reason.[1] After a few months I spoke with a wise monk who said to me, "Everything we do, we do for a dozen or more reasons. If you waited for every one of those reasons to be good you'd never do anything. If *one* of those reasons is good, God can work with that, don't you worry." It remains some of the best and most liberating advice I've ever been given.

Paul isn't all that worried about mixed motives. I'm not sure we should be a whole lot more worried than Paul was. In a world where there are tax incentives for charitable giving and naming opportunities for institutional donors, it's a fantasy that we'll ever get to a place where the left hand is totally unaware of what the right hand is doing. Our conscience may never be completely clear and our intentions seldom entirely noble. But we can still try to be faithful disciples in the financial part of our lives. So how do we work out what, where, and how to give? I want to suggest three dimensions to giving.

The first is *giving with your head*. Giving with your head is about sticking to the three Rs of financial giving.

R number one is *routine*. By all means investigate causes of the social ills nonprofits seek to address. By all means investigate the organizations you're considering giving money to, for their purpose, probity, plans, and personnel. But in the end, giving is about regular

---

1. "The last temptation is the greatest treason: To do the right deed for the wrong reason." T. S. Eliot, *Murder in the Cathedral* (New York: Harcourt Brace Jovanovich, 1963), 44.

habits, not grand gestures. Paul says, "As you excel in everything, excel in generosity." It's often said that time is money. But it's less often realized that money is time. Managing money takes enormous amounts of time, whether you have a little or a lot, and in the end most people who have a lot get others to do it for them. Giving is the same. Find the right organizations and leave the details to them. If at all possible, don't save all the checks until December. Become the kind of donor organizations rely on. Whatever the amount you give, give monthly as a matter of routine.

R number two is *realism*. Take an honest assessment of what you can give and try to stick to it. Paul says, "If the eagerness is there, the gift is acceptable according to what one has" (2 Cor. 8:12). The reason poorer people tend to give more than richer people is that richer people are usually more "careful" with their money. (They might say that's why they're rich, after all!) Realism means you might sometimes have to say no. But that no is because you've said yes to a need elsewhere. Realism also means anticipating that crises and disasters will occur for you and for others, and thus means keeping something back for such moments. But realism isn't just for people on tight budgets. I know one well-off person who says that in tight financial times it is for those who can still give generously to make up for those who currently can't. That's what I call eager realism.

R number three is *relationships*. There are things money can't do and things money makes worse. We've probably all had a friendship that's gone wrong somehow over the giving or lending of money. While giving money should become routine and be realistic, we should always remember that money is for making relationships and relationships are never for making money. Paul's plea to the Corinthians is not to their wallets but to their common baptism with the Jerusalem Christians. He's saying, "It's time to show what being one body means." Our fundamental need for relationship is more profound than our need for money. In the face of another's distress we're best not leading with the checkbook and saying, "This is what I'd like to do for you"—but asking the gentle question, "How do you need me to be with you?"

Those are the three Rs of giving with your head.

The second dimension of giving is *giving with your hand*.

86

Paul says, "Finish doing what you began." It's all very well sorting out all the rights and wrongs in your head, but it doesn't amount to much if you don't get around to writing and sending the check. Giving with your hand means recognizing there'll always be something untidy about giving but that's not a reason not to do it. But giving with your hand also means combining money with action. You can't entirely subcontract kindness and generosity. At some stage there needs to be face-to-face encounter, genuine human warmth, touch, and interaction.

That's one of the biggest reasons churches go on mission trips. Yes, they often do useful work erecting homes, dispensing medications, and clearing flood debris. But a lot of what they're about is being the human face of the checkbook. It's saying to people, "We know you're facing hardship. We want to be helpful. We're used to avoiding your gaze and just sending money, but this week we want to see, touch, and embrace you in your humanity and ours, to look you in the eye even if you or we find it hard not to look away in shame or embarrassment, to hear your anger, listen to your despair, and affirm your hope."

Giving with your hand means seeing for yourself what money can and can't do. It means coming home from the mission trip or the night shelter with a deeper understanding of what it feels like to be the recipient of charity, what it feels like to know when you're not meeting people's deepest needs, and what it can mean to be a small part of a person finding their own way to get on their feet again. Giving with your hand informs the way you spend your money and transforms the way you pray.

Finally, there's the third dimension of giving: *giving with your heart*.

More than once Paul says giving is about turning your eagerness into tangible contributions. A lot of us are very protective when it comes to giving with our heart. We're cynical about emotional appeals featuring wide-eyed infants looking doleful and hungry. We're wary of the sentimentality that assumes the world's problems would evaporate if we just wrote that check. And we're frightened of entering into financial commitments where we could be taken advantage of or personal relationships where we could find ourselves out of our depth.

But we all know Paul's most famous words from 1 Corinthians 13. "If I give away all my possessions, and if I hand over my body so that I may boast, but do not have love, I gain nothing." Just as you can't entirely subcontract generosity, you can't entirely subcontract the emotional side of giving either. We think God wants us to give to others because God could use a little help from us in changing their lives. But the real reason God wants us to give to others is to change *our* lives. Fundamentally that's the difference between giving with your head and hand, and giving with your heart. Giving with your head and hand changes others. Giving with your heart changes you. There are a hundred reasons why you may not want to do it, but allowing yourself to be changed by a relationship is in the end what giving really means.

Probably none of us are equally adept at giving with our head, hand, and heart. That's one of the many reasons we need one another. If you look across your lifetime, it could be that as an elderly person you feel it's harder to give with your hand than it once was. As a parent of young children trying to hold down a demanding job it may be harder to give with your heart. As a young teenager it might be harder to give with your head. We're all different in personality and in our season of life.

That's why giving isn't fundamentally a private matter. That's why giving corporately as a church is so important. Churches aren't oceans of peace and tranquility—they're more often places of sustained argument. And one of the best arguments you can have in a church is what to give money to, because it's only when we get into that kind of argument that we work out whether the gospel is fundamentally about head, hand, or heart. Of course it's about all of these things. But it's only when we're forced to make decisions together about things we all think matter—like our money—that we discover the full implications of the gospel. Left to ourselves we'd fall back into whichever comes easiest—head, hand, or heart. But thrown together as one body we discover that the gospel means all three. We need the church because it's just not possible for any of us to grasp the whole gospel on our own.

And that's why the most beautiful and most challenging of Paul's words in 2 Corinthians are these: "You know the generous act of our Lord Jesus Christ, that though he was rich, yet for your sakes he became poor, so that by his poverty you might become rich" (2 Cor. 8:9). In other words, the way Jesus makes room for *us* in *his* life is by emptying himself of everything else. When we enter his life we become rich beyond measure. And so the way *we* make room for Jesus in *our* life is by emptying ourselves of what is there. The more we give, the more room we make for Jesus. Thus the poorer we become, the more we are open to being filled by the riches of the Holy Spirit.

So the question for us becomes not, "How much shall we give, and to whom, and how often, and how can we be sure they'll spend it wisely?" The question finally becomes, "How much room in our lives have we made to be filled with Jesus?" After all, he has emptied his life to be filled with us.

In the end, our heads, our hands, and our hearts are given to us for one reason above all: that we may open them out to others, in such a way that they may be filled with Jesus Christ.

# 14

# Is There a Gospel for the Rich?

Is there a gospel for the rich? When I was at seminary a wise colleague who had formerly been a high school teacher advised me on how to tackle my assignments. He said, "There are always three answers to every question: 'yes,' 'no,' and 'maybe'—and the answer is nearly always 'maybe.'" Is there a gospel for the rich? The answer the New Testament gives to this question seems to be "maybe." To say "no" implies there's something inherently dirty about money. It suggests that every cent the rich have is taken directly out of the pockets of the poor. It seems to represent a kind of anger that assumes that what God really wants is for everyone to be miserable. But simply to say "yes" is to ignore the pasting the rich seem to get in the four Gospels, especially Luke. It's easier for a camel to pass through the eye of a needle, remember, than for a rich person to enter the kingdom of God. No one can serve God and Mammon. And in Luke 12, we have a parable in which a rich man says to himself, "What shall I do, for I have no place to store my crops? . . . I will pull down my barns and build larger ones" (vv. 17–18). And God calls him an idiot and takes his life the very same night. So the answer to the question "Is there a gospel for the rich?" has to be "maybe." Today I want to explore some of the questions raised by that "maybe."

Let's start with the parable. The things the rich man gets wrong set the agenda for all our thinking about wealth and its pitfalls. First of all the rich man forgets God because he assumes all his wealth belongs to him and that he will possess it indefinitely. It turns out his wealth is in fact on loan from God, and God can have it back at any moment. This is a slap in the face for any view of society that prizes private property. Notice how the rich man likes the word *my*. In Jesus's parable, when the rich man notices that his land has produced abundantly, he thinks to himself, "What should I do, for I have no place to store my crops? . . . I will do this: I will pull down my barns and build larger ones, and there I will store all my grain and my goods. And I will say to my soul, Soul, you have ample goods laid up for many years; relax, eat, drink, be merry" (Luke 12:17–19). *My* crops, *my* barns, *my* grain, *my* goods, *my* soul, he says, all in the space of a couple of verses. But the parable makes it clear that all these things have been God's all along, and the rich man only ever has them out on loan. Abundance turns to greed the moment the rich man forgets that everything he has belongs all along to God.

And the second thing the rich man forgets is anyone else but himself. Instead of pausing at the point when he has more than enough, and wondering who else might welcome a little bit more, he presses on and builds bigger barns. And it turns out that the conversations he should have been having with friends and neighbors, the wise and the needy, he is in fact having just with himself. "He thought to himself," says the parable, and then again, "He said to himself." Abundance turns to greed the moment the rich man assumes wealth exists to insulate him from other people rather than to draw him closer to them. This parable shows us what greed is. Greed strives for more without asking what the more is for. Greed is so dazzled by the potential of what money can do that it is content to accumulate without ever investing. Greed stops seeing money as a means to an end and instead sees wealth as an end in itself.

Is it wrong to be rich? This parable doesn't say so, but it does offer a very straightforward account of how difficult it is to be rich and to be faithful: wealth inclines us to forget God and forget other people. Let's start with God. When we have a lot of money, it is easy to make the assumption that money can solve pretty much all our irritations and frustrations. Don't like vacuuming? Pay someone to clean our house. Think our children could get a better education? Pay for one. Not impressed with our health care? Pay for a second opinion. Find long journeys tedious? Buy a nicer car with a purring stereo or—even better—acquire a private jet. It begins to seem like there's nothing money can't buy. Except of course the things that really matter. There's nothing wrong with being rich so long as we remember that. Money can't buy eternal life. Money can't buy the forgiveness of sins. Money can't buy the faith that moves mountains. Money can't buy the hope that walks in rhythm with God's step. Money can't buy the love that will not let us go. These are things that everyone can have but no one can buy. The poor are blessed because, on the whole, they know this. The rich can sometimes become a little forgetful.

And when it comes to other people, wealth can have a poisoning effect. If we have no possessions, other people are all we have, and we're well advised to keep on pretty good terms with them because we know we're going to need them sooner rather than later, as soon as anything goes wrong. But if we have great wealth, great property, and great possessions, other people can quickly stop being potential friends and even saviors, and on the contrary become potential threats and enemies who could rob or steal what we have. Instead of looking at friends with hope we start to look at strangers with fear. Quickly we start to defend our property with alarms and fences and big dogs, and we find we can't trust anybody because everyone we meet wants something from us. We get further and further away from real human contact with the people whom we pay to make our life better, and it gets harder and harder to make genuine relationships and friendships with them or indeed anybody. So of course we find it difficult to imagine sharing our surplus income with anyone else because we've avoided getting to know personally anyone who could in any way represent a threat to our insulated wealth. This is how wealth can make us forget God and thus live in a fantasy of our own immortality, and also can make us forget other people and thus live in a prison of our own self-sufficiency. This is exactly what Jesus is striving to save us from, and he does it bluntly by calling the rich man a fool—an idiot.

So there's a lot of bad news for the rich in this parable, and it's not just bad news in the hereafter; it's just as much bad news in the here and now—bad news that says wealth can put us in a fantasyland at best and a prison at worst. So what's the good news? Is there a gospel for the rich? Maybe there is. But to find it, we need to ask some searching and pretty fundamental questions. And the key question is this: what is money for? The rich man in the parable thought money was for accumulating and enjoying. There's an interesting Greek word here for "enjoying"—*euphoria*. The rich man thought money was for euphoria. But I suggest money is for something else. Money is a mechanism by which human societies translate labor into other things. Money is of no value in itself: it only becomes valuable when it is translated into other things. And the word we use for that translation is *investment*.

We usually use the word *investment* for any method of accumulating money. Any way we devise to increase our wealth we tend to call an investment. But I'd like us to think for a moment of the word *investment* as referring not just to the accumulation of wealth but also to every single use to which we put money. In other words, I want to break down the conventional distinction between money we keep and money we give away, and instead suggest that we think of the various things we can do with money as different kinds of investment. We are rich if we find that, after working out what we need to eat and clothe and shelter ourselves and our dependents, we have money left over. If that is our situation, I suggest there are about five things we can do with our remaining money, and I want to quickly run through them now, to show the difference between investment and mere accumulation, and thus offer a gospel for the rich by suggesting what it might mean to become "rich toward God" (Luke 12:21).

The first thing we can do with money is give it away to individuals. Somehow when we hear Jesus telling the rich young man, "Go, sell what you have, give to the poor and come follow me," we imagine some kind of random distribution of wads of banknotes. Giving large sums of money to individuals is generally a very poor investment. For most people who are poor, lack of money isn't the only, or even the main, problem. A sudden influx of unearned cash may do a whole lot more harm than good, particularly if it comes without genuine relationship or appropriate human understanding. The gospel for the rich does not mean an unthinking throwing of money at the poor. As for aid agencies and similar nonprofits and NGOs, it's common to complain that such organizations generate high administrative overheads. But that assumes it's possible to give to the poor in a nonwasteful way. I'm not sure it is. Sometimes the overheads can be excessive, and that's often a sign the organization is getting something seriously wrong. But in general, the overheads are the money we pay in order to ensure our gifts to the poor are distributed wisely.

A second thing we can do with money is to give it to institutions established and governed in such a way that they have a time-honored record of turning money into real human value, in education, health, the practice and sharing of faith, the arts, or a host of other forms. Institution-building is generally a wonderful investment, because it turns the potential of money into the reality of human flourishing, both now and in the future. The best of these institutions have a close eye for how their work genuinely benefits the poor in ways that don't reinforce the cycles, patterns, and habits of poverty. This is one of the finest things we do with our money in order not to build bigger barns but to become rich toward God.

A third and more controversial thing we must do with our money is to yield much of it up to our local and national governments in taxes. The government is an institution or an aggregate of institutions designed, among other things, to turn money into real human value. Its main difference from the institutions previously mentioned is the relatively small degree of choice we get over where our money goes. But it needs to be said that paying taxes is an honorable thing, that an important part of being rich is about paying a lot of tax, and that paying a lot of tax is something to be proud of and not something to avoid at all costs through fiscal loopholes and offshore accounts. Taxes are a way of making sure surplus money is invested in public good rather than accumulated for private gain. Government is seldom a highly efficient mechanism for investment, and at times it looks like a bigger barn all of its own, but we must be clear that paying proportionate amounts of tax is part of the gospel for the rich.

The fourth thing many people with money to spare do with that money is establish more conventional investments, such as stocks and shares. While this is a very common way to store up treasure for ourselves, it is a very risky way to become rich toward God, precisely because of the temptation to accumulate and forever postpone the moment when the wealth is translated into genuine human value. As Jesus says right before he tells the parable about the rich man and his barns, "Be on your guard against all kinds of greed; for one's life does not consist in the abundance of possessions" (Luke 12:15). However, there are two exceptions to this risk. One is to become an active shareholder, agitating for the companies we partly own to embody best practice in their production, marketing, employment, and environmental impact, and in all appropriate ways to exercise their corporate power for the wider social good. Indeed, I believe it is almost a duty for those who are rich to seek to influence the business world for good in this way. The second exception that can make conventional investors rich toward God is to allow their capital to be used for social good. For example, community development finance initiatives operate just like a bank, with market-level interest rates, but they use their capital to loan money to enable people on low incomes to buy property or start up their own enterprises. Investing in community development finance initiatives is a way for the wealthy to become rich toward God because it means entering a world in which everyone can benefit from their wealth.

The fifth and final use of money is to acquire property and possessions. It's amazing how many rich people live very simply, whether out of distaste for ostentation, or to be free of the prison of possessions, or to avoid facing the visible manifestation of their own wealth. If one is to become rich toward God, it's important that such simple living represents true freedom from greed and not tightfisted miserliness or straightforward denial. But there's no doubt that great temptation lies in accumulating property and possessions. To address such temptation, I suggest asking ourselves the following kinds of questions about what we own.

- How reluctant am I to lend my possessions to others? (Willingness to be generous is a pretty good indication of how much you recognize everything you have is ultimately on loan from God.)

- Am I constantly looking out for ways in which others can enjoy what I own, or are my possessions a wall that insulates me from the strange and dangerous outside world?
- Do my enjoyment, my flourishing, and my entertainment co-incide with the joy of others, or does it come at others' expense?
- Does my wealth make me and others free, or does it make me and others a prisoner?
- Do I fundamentally want the things that everyone else can have as well?
- And finally, am I prepared to allow others to free me from self-deception by sharing the truth about my financial situation with members of my church and asking for their prayers and guidance?

These are the questions that test whether you are becoming rich toward God.

I want to finish with one of my favorite stories, which is about faith, but, like the parable in Luke 12, could also be about money. I want us to think about what God is saying to us through this story. A man fell off a cliff and tumbled down into a ravine, falling helplessly until he just managed to grab on to the branch of a tree growing out of the rock face. Dangling from the branch, and holding on with all his might, he shouted up to the top of the cliff, "Is anybody up there who could help me?" After a short pause a voice came from below him, "My son, I am here. Let go of the branch and I will catch you." The man thought for a while, and then he shouted up again, "Is there anybody up there?"

# 15

# The Education of Desire

I was born into a culture that was very suspicious of power. There could be lots of reasons for this. It could be because all power is said to corrupt. It could be because this was the sixties, a time when white males stopped being seen as the source of all good and started being seen by many as the cause of all evil. But I think it was because powerful people tend either to seek or to find that they become the center of attention, and, in the culture in which I was raised, being the center of attention was considered very bad manners. The way to show you were well behaved was to let the other child win, never to exaggerate, and always to remember that people in Africa were having a terrible time (so one could never complain)—and, eager to please, that was exactly what I did.

The trouble with this form of good manners is that it becomes very difficult to talk about the power of God. Power seems at best a necessary evil, so one can't imagine God having any. Sure, Jesus suffers uncomplainingly; sure he stands alongside those who struggle for justice; sure he dies in agony on the cross. But the miracles and the divinity and the resurrection become a bit harder to talk about. They seem to make Jesus the center of attention. They seem somehow impolite.

But this is to make the story of Jesus no more than a genteel account of how violence, selfishness, and fear always win. And this misses the heart of the gospel. The heart of the gospel is that Jesus was raised from the dead. This is a unique act of power that shows us definitively the nature of God. The resurrection of Jesus is both forward-looking and backward-looking. It gives us a new future because it means that death is not the end, and it shows us the eternal life that God has in store for us. It gives us a new past because it shows that every failure and sin and catastrophe, even the cross itself, can be and has been redeemed, and so every aspect of our lives can be ransomed, healed, restored, and forgiven. The cross and resurrection is the center of history because it gives us a new future and restores our past. That's the heart of the gospel.

If cross and resurrection are the center of history, then our notion of power is transformed. What's wrong with violence is not that its weapons are too strong and they threaten to destroy God's reign, but on the contrary that its weapons are too weak and they distract from where true power lies. What's wrong with injustice is not that it sets up barriers that will never be overcome but that it pathetically tries to push back the tidal wave of righteousness that will flow like a never-failing stream. Violence and injustice cause untold suffering, but the good news of the resurrection is that their power is as nothing before the power of God.

This is the most important part of the gospel, but it's also the most difficult part. We want the gospel to end with the resurrection so we can all live happily ever after. But it doesn't end with the resurrection. It carries on. It makes its way through the challenges, failures, and struggles of the early church and all the way up to our present day. Now the Gospel of Luke tells us that we're not the only ones who find the existence of suffering and injustice the hardest part of the gospel. Jesus seems to have found it difficult as well. Just look at the temptations he faced in the desert.

Jesus goes into the wilderness after his baptism, just as Israel went into the wilderness after crossing the Red Sea. And he goes there to find out the same thing Israel went to find out: what it means to have power.

The first temptation he faces is about physical power. He's surrounded by stones, and it would make life a whole lot easier if he were to turn one of them into a loaf of bread. But he doesn't, because he is learning what it means to have power over his own body. Yes, he's hungry, but that doesn't mean he allows hunger to take over his imagination so he can't think of anything else. Yes, he could do with some coffee, but he's not going to let his body become subject to a craving for caffeine before he can embark on any form of physical effort or serious thought. Yes, he'd love a beer, but he's finding ways to relax and be cheerful and find a sense of humor without depending on a brown bottle to do it all for him. Yes, he'd love to be intimate and feel the sexual excitement of holding somebody close, but he's here in the wilderness to learn not to be subject to the whim of lust and the sovereignty of his hormones. Yes, he's tired, but he's discovering that he can't make sleepiness a perpetual excuse for avoiding those things he doesn't want to do, and he can't make his own exhaustion a symbol of his self-importance.

What he does is to transform every desire into a desire for God. "One does not live by bread alone," says Jesus (Matt. 4:4; Luke 4:4; quoting Deut. 8:3), and goes on to say, "but by every word that proceeds from the mouth of God." If he had bread, he'd be hungry the next day. If he had a beer, he'd be thirsty again. But learning to desire the word of God, learning to feed on the bread of heaven, means he'll never be hungry again. That's power.

The second temptation Jesus faces is a political one. Here he is, out in the wilderness, a long way from making the kind of difference in Israel and the world that the angels and the magi talked about at his birth. And the devil shows Jesus all the kingdoms of the world and offers them to him, saying, "To you I will give their glory and all this authority." This is the chance to set right injustice, to end violence, to legislate the kingdom of God. But Jesus doesn't take the offer because he's learning where true power lies. Governments are important. They influence most people's lives. But one can become obsessed about public office and the personalities in the public spotlight. Just imagine what power one might discover if one set that aside for a moment: the power of wisdom; the power of truth; the power of the soil, seas, air, wind, and sun; the power of ideas; the power of the imagination; the power of rhetoric; and the power of knowledge. Jesus says there's one thing that's always more important than government, and that's worship. For worship directs you to where true power lies, a power that government can only envy.

Jesus transforms the desire to control into the desire to worship. Rather than be determined to be in charge of everything, Jesus reorients our gaze to the one who really is in charge. He says, quoting Deuteronomy 6:13, "Worship the Lord your God, and serve only him" (Matt. 4:10; Luke 4:8). The only true government is founded on true worship. That's power.

The third temptation Jesus faces is a supernatural one. The devil whisks Jesus away to Jerusalem, places him on the pinnacle of the temple, and dares Jesus to throw himself down, saying, "For it is written, 'He will command his angels concerning you, to protect you,' and 'On their hands they will bear you up, so that you will not dash your foot against a stone'" (Luke 4:10–11; quoting Ps. 91:11, 12). We're all captivated by the thrill of fantasy, lured by the promise of magic, enticed by the prospect of a spectacle. That's why we're drawn to the television, sucked into the world of major league sports, and fascinated by celebrity. They each offer us an instant prospect of a magic carpet to another world of heroes and conquests and drama and delight—a world so much more entertaining than our ordinary one. But Jesus isn't interested in a fantasy world. He's not dazzled by popularity, celebrity, admiration, or even headline news. He's in the wilderness to learn those things that really bring change. His ministry isn't going to be about playing games with God.

Jesus takes the desire for titillation and turns it into the desire for transformation. He's not going to be distracted by the exciting, the spectacular, or the intriguing. He can't be bought off with food; he can't be fobbed off with high office; he can't be distracted by entertainment. He can't be put off from his purpose. That's power.

Only after Jesus has discovered where power truly lies is he ready to exercise his own power. Jesus discovers that there is more to wish for than simply feeding a hungry world, much as he and we would love to. Many Christians who have followed Jesus have fallen for this first temptation. But the truth is that the world whose hunger was satisfied this way would tomorrow simply be hungry again. Jesus discovers that there is more to wish for than ruling the world, much as he and we might wish to. Many Christians who have followed Jesus have fallen for this second temptation. But the truth is that governments don't finally rule the world: they come and go, while God's rule, encountered and celebrated in worship, never comes to an end. Jesus discovers that there is more to wish for than excitement and drama, much as he and we enjoy it. Many Christians who have followed Jesus have fallen for this third temptation. But the truth is such things are most often a distraction from the transformation Jesus truly brings.

The irony of course is that Jesus did feed people, by turning five loaves into food for five thousand. He does rule the world, crowned with thorns on Good Friday and enthroned in glory on Ascension Day. And he does employ a company of angels, to roll away the stone on Easter. But he only does those things after he has discovered what true power is and where true power lies. And the same goes for us. Of course we seek to feed a hungry world. Of course we seek to make a more just world through the offices of government. And of course we enjoy bringing drama and excitement to the world through entertainment, sports, and the media. But first we must discover what true power is and where true power lies.

And that is what the practices of discipleship—habits like keeping Sabbath, holding to a regular discipline of prayer, shaping your life around Sunday worship, reading the Bible devotionally and corporately, giving money sacrificially, fasting carefully, and focusing on all such disciplines for seven weeks each year during Lent—are for. Discipline is for discovering what true power is and where true power lies. Discovering what true power is means educating our desires. That's the point of giving things up for Lent, and the point of discipline throughout the year. Just as an athlete or soldier or musician undergoes a rigorous discipline of training to make sure they can do the right thing at the right time and never fall back on the excuse of not feeling like it or having a bad day, just so through fasting or other intentional self-renunciation Christians discipline their bodies so they are ready to respond to God's call whenever it may come. You fast so that you learn to hear the call of God louder than the call of the refrigerator. You train your body, your senses, your imagination so you learn to do what God wants you to do rather than what advertisers, seducers, or tempters want you to do. This is true power.

But true power doesn't ultimately lie in our bodies, willpower, or mental strength. True power lies in God, the resurrection of Jesus

101

Christ, the forgiveness and healing of the past, and the wondrous promise of an eternal future that Jesus's resurrection brings. The practices and disciplines of discipleship aren't just to train our hearts and minds to be ready to act in the right way. These are times for reorienting our awareness to where true power lies.

There are many times of preparation in our lives. One of the most obvious is the time many young people spend at university. While it's not common to think of them in such a way, four undergraduate years at college can be a kind of Lent. They're a time of preparation. They're a time when students leave the familiarity of their home-towns and go to a strange place for a period to make them ready to use power. They're also a time of developing the body, mind, and spirit, of learning what to desire and how, of forming disciplines and discovering wisdom and truth. Most obviously, they're a time of training for the roles and offices of responsibility and influence in society. But if this is a time of growing in power, it's important to ensure it is spent discovering what true power is and where true power lies. Those who never went to college or look back on their college years over the shoulder of many years' subsequent experience may ruefully reflect that there's no better opportunity than college years for discovering where true power lies.

My prayer for my undergraduate friends is this: that during their four years in college they become people of power—people who know what true power is and where true power lies. True power must involve becoming a person who can't be bought off with food, can't be fobbed off with high office, and can't be distracted by entertainment. True power must involve being ready for God. If you are such a person, you'll be a person of power. But true power ultimately lies not in shaping our desire for God but in realizing God's desire for us. And God's desire for us is enfleshed in the life, death, and resurrection of Jesus. May all our strivings in discipleship be an experience of developing our own power, fostering that power in others, and meeting true power in the God of Jesus Christ.

# be not afraid of difference

God the Holy Trinity is three in one and one in three. God did not need to create the universe, but without creation we would not have known God.

These are the two central claims of Christian faith that sustain it in the face of the challenges that cluster around the theme of "difference." Christianity began among the poor but has often seemed to be the possession of the privileged classes. It began among what are sometimes called "people of color" but has often seemed to belong to Western Europeans and members of the North European diaspora. It has always been characterized greatly or largely by women but has often been controlled by men. Once these facts are recognized, the whole gospel—or at least the church—seems sometimes to be in jeopardy.

But God is three in one and one in three. There was diversity from before the beginning. And that diversity is intrinsically harmonious. Diversity does not in itself cause or provoke conflict. Harmony is more basic than disharmony. Harmony is in the heart of God, and the heart of God is plural.

Meanwhile, God made the universe. The universe was from the beginning different from God and diverse within itself. And God saw that it was good. Creation was the establishment of difference as peace.[1] Even the existence of the eternal God alongside the temporal universe was a companionship of peace.

These twin convictions inspire Christians in the face of challenges and misgivings about unequal distribution of power and opportunity and in some cases the shameful history of the church in regard to issues of difference. Difference is real. It is good. It can be misused and exploited. It can not only be redeemed but more often can itself be the source of redemption. These are the principles that underlie the following reflections.

1. This sentence is inspired by John Milbank's words, "Christianity . . . is the coding of transcendental difference as peace" in *Theology and Social Theory: Beyond Secular Reason* (Cambridge, MA: Blackwell, 1990), 5–6.

# 16

# You Are Not Your Own

It's become common in America for people to come together one weekend a year in churches and other meeting places to reflect about the issue of race in this country. We do so in the name of Martin Luther King Jr., the person who above all others pointed to a vision in which children would grow to be judged not by the color of their skin but by the content of their character.

It seems to be taken for granted in some circles that the one invited to speak on these occasions should be an African American. Though this is understandable, I have begun to wonder whether such an assumption still serves this nation's common destiny. It seems to suggest that black people know what race is in a way white people don't—as if somehow black people *have* race while white people don't because white people represent some kind of primeval default setting from which other races differ in varying degrees. But this is nonsense—race is something everyone has, and it's a significant part of anyone's identity because it's not subject to change.

There are those who want to downplay the historic injustice and present imbalance in the relation of black and white in this country by setting it in a wider context of the assimilation of a host of races and nationalities into this nation's culture, or even going wider and looking to the mutual hospitality, understanding, and appreciation of many kinds of difference ranging from class to disability to sexual orientation, all under the general and apparently infinitely malleable label of diversity. In this spirit it has sometimes been said that Martin Luther King Jr. died and rose again as a white liberal, because his legacy has somehow been hitched to a ragbag of causes about which he expressed no public view. But to my mind this observation, while sharp, also misses the key point.

The key point is easily discovered by simply picking up a dictionary (or going online and consulting Wikipedia). Read some of the entries under "Black": "thoroughly sinister or evil"; "indicative of condemnation or discredit"; "very sad, gloomy, or calamitous."[1] "Common connotations" for the word *black* are said to include: "darkness, secrecy, death, fear, antagonist, chaos, evil, bad luck, crime." And, "Black magic is a destructive or evil form of magic, often connected with death. . . . Evil witches are stereotypically dressed in black."[2] And then flip some pages or click again and read some of the entries for "White": "marked by upright fairness"; "free from spot or blemish . . . free from moral impurity"; "not intended to cause harm."[3] The color white commonly represents "purity, snow, ice, peace, nobility, God, clean air, heaven, peace. . . . White is the color worn by brides at weddings. . . . Angels are typically depicted as clothed in white robes."[4] *The Free Dictionary* adds, "Someone who is whiter than white is completely good and honest and never does anything bad."[5] I don't think there's much more that needs to be said. The characterization of those with pink or peach colored skin as white and therefore pure, and those of dark brown skin as black and therefore frightening and chaotic, runs so deep in our culture that it still permeates twenty-first-century dictionaries.

So if we ask, what is the question of race really about? here's a simple answer. A black person in the English-speaking world, even in the unlikely event that they've never been racially abused,

---

1. *Merriam-Webster's Collegiate Dictionary*, 11th ed. (Springfield, MA: Merriam-Webster, 2003), 127.

2. *Wikipedia*, s.v. "Black," http://en.wikipedia.org/wiki/Black.

3. *Merriam-Webster's Collegiate Dictionary*, 1427.

4. *Wikipedia*, s.v. "White," http://en.wikipedia.org/wiki/White.

5. *The Free Dictionary*, s.v. "White," http://idioms.thefreedictionary.com/white.

discriminated against, excluded, or humiliated, still picks up any dictionary and finds the weight of culture a burden on their shoulders and the incline on the dial of social standing set to permanently uphill. But as Christians, when we ask, what is the question of race really about? we can't be content with sociological answers. We want *theo*logical answers. What's the problem? In what ways does Jesus address the problem? How does the church witness to the way Jesus has addressed the problem? These are the three key questions.

What's the problem of racism? Most of us are familiar with a distressing catalog of symptoms—but what exactly is the root cause? We could simply say "sin"—but precisely what *kind* of sin? Time and again the book of Genesis presents us with the stories of siblings competing, often for their parents' attention. There's Cain and Abel, Isaac and Ishmael, Jacob and Esau, and Joseph and pretty well everybody. Sibling rivalry is so profound a feature of Genesis that it somehow sets its mark over the whole Bible, so that Paul sets the relationship of Israel and the gentiles, the most significant one of all for the early church, in the context of these ancient sibling rivalries. And what is sibling rivalry fundamentally about? It's about fearing that there won't be enough for everybody. There won't be enough resources and there won't be enough love. So I'm going to dominate my sibling, by fair means or foul, lest I end up on the losing side. Isn't the story of the white and the black races over the last five hundred years like a kind of sibling rivalry *by groups*? By fair means or foul, one sibling has grasped the heel of the other, done whatever it took to steal the inheritance—because fundamentally it feared there wouldn't be enough for both. The dominant sibling then created an ideology of supremacy, superiority, and lurking crisis that enculturated its advantage and demonized anyone who might possibly alter the status quo. But the root of the sin is allowing ourselves to believe that there isn't enough for everyone. And so in the face of the person who's different from us not by language or class or creed but by race, a difference almost impossible to alter, we either ignore the other, subjugate them, demonize them, or destroy them. Unless . . . unless we truly believe there's enough for everyone of the things that really matter.

This is how Jesus addresses the problem. He says to those on opposing sides of the dividing wall of hostility, there *is* enough for

107

everyone. He calls all kinds of people to be disciples; he makes five loaves feed five thousand people; his forgiveness endures even crucifixion; his life cannot be destroyed even by death; his Spirit speaks to everyone in their own language; his gospel goes to the ends of the earth. In all these ways Jesus displays that the true gifts of God—life, love, forgiveness, resurrection, the Holy Spirit—*these* are gifts that never run out. They're not in short supply. The more we share them, the more of them there is.

Meanwhile Jesus blows away two of the fundamental myths that underpin racist ideology. First of all, there's no such thing as racial purity. Life is not a dog show, with our owners parading our pedigree before the judges. We're all mutts. Jesus over and over again displaced a theory of salvation based on purity in favor of a salvation based on repentance, conversion, and forgiveness. There's no entitlement in the kingdom of God. Heaven is not restricted.

And second, the way we're made is not the most fundamental thing in God's eyes. Race and gender, the two most apparently indelible characteristics, are important and precious, but they're not *fundamental* to the way God sees our identity. God's not actually all that concerned about what you are and where you're coming from. He's concerned about who you're becoming and where you're going. Remember St. Paul wasn't a white guy. His life changed on the Damascus Road. That day he discovered it's not about race, it's about grace. That became his message: it's not about race, it's about grace. Our identity as Christians rests solely in this: our baptism. It's our baptism that turns us from the exiles, mongrels, sinners, and strangers that we are into a chosen race, a royal priesthood, a holy nation, God's own people. If we are really reading the New Testament right, when we fill in the questionnaire that says "Nationality" we'd write "Christian," and the one that says "Race" we'd again have nothing more or less to say than, simply, "Christian." We each have many characteristics, but one stands out above all others. And that's baptism. For Christians, it's not about race, it's about grace.

At a conference in Chicago in 1963 to mark the one hundredth anniversary of the Emancipation Proclamation, one speaker began his address with the words, "The issue, the only *issue*, at this conference is baptism." The delegates rose to their feet in outrage at the offense to Jews and secular activists who were treasured members of the civil rights movement. As one observer noted, "Nothing can be more hostile and boisterous than 657 liberals bent on solving someone else's problem when the harmony and unanimity of the occasion is threatened."[6] Dr. King was a genius at building a movement that could bind together people of a host of different persuasions and commitments to address a common enemy. But he was a Baptist pastor, and he, better than anyone, knew that for Christians, no science, no account of tolerance, no desire for progress, no program of education, no call for common humanity can finally achieve what Christ brings about in baptism. Baptism doesn't abolish difference—but it transforms difference from a cause for fear into a manifestation of abundance.

So this is how Jesus addresses the problem of racism: he dismantles and discredits the myths of purity and nature that make racism plausible, and he displaces the ideology of scarcity that makes racism credible. Racism is exposed as a logic of fear that rests on the assumption that the God of Jesus Christ does not exist. Racism is about finding a security and an identity other than the security and identity found in God. It is, in the end, a form of atheism.

And so our response to racism, in ourselves and in others, personally and corporately, prophetically and institutionally, is vital to our witness to the God of Jesus Christ. As Paul says to the Corinthians, "Your body is a temple of the Holy Spirit. . . . You are not your own" (1 Cor. 6:19). God gives us to one another as places of encounter, as temples through whom we can encounter the Holy Spirit. That's what we are each *for*. To dismiss or oppress people of another race out of hand is to deny oneself access to God's Holy Spirit, the Spirit that God communicates to us through them. *They* lose from our cruelty, but *we* lose even more because we're deprived

6. The gathering was the January 14–17, 1963, National Conference on Race and Religion, jointly sponsored by the National Catholic Welfare Conference, the National Council of Churches, and the Synagogue Council of America. The speaker in question was William Stringfellow. For his address, see Stringfellow, "Care Enough to Weep" (draft manuscript of address at the National Conference on Religion and Race in Chicago, January 14–17, 1963, box 7, William Stringfellow Papers, #4438, Department of Manuscripts and University Archives, Cornell University Library), 2. The account and the observation quoted may be found in Will D. Campbell, *Brother to a Dragonfly* (New York: Continuum, 2000), 230. See also Marshall Ron Johnston, *Bombast, Blasphemy, and the Bastard Gospel: William Stringfellow and American Exceptionalism* (PhD dissertation, Baylor University, 2007), 62–66.

of the place where God promises to encounter us. Our assumption of scarcity rebounds back on ourselves. Racism simply gives us less access to God.

But racism is nonetheless still with us and in us. So finally I want to say a few words about how the church *witnesses* to the way Jesus has addressed the problem. Christians of different races need one another to hear everything God has to tell us in Scripture. How can we hear the story of the matriarch Sarah and the slave Hagar if we have never known anyone like Sarah or Hagar? How can we hear the story of Moses if no one among us has any idea what it means to say "let my people go"? How can we hear the story of Daniel or Esther if no one among us has ever known what it means to be in charge of a nation or organization and still be regarded in that nation or organization as a second-class citizen? How are we to hear the words "Can anything good come out of Nazareth?" if no one among us has come from humble and despised origins? We approach Christians of histories and locations different from our own, and one of the first things we say is, "Help me to hear what God is saying in the Bible." God has given us in Jesus and the Holy Spirit everything we need to live beyond racism—but we need to receive everything God's given us, and that means receiving one another's unique and different experience and wisdom.

One slogan that was much circulated during the 2008 US presidential election went like this: "Rosa sat so that Martin could walk. Martin walked so that Barack could run." I think this slogan has a great deal to teach the church. It says that each act or gesture of courage, faith, or defiance takes its place in a litany of such acts, most of which remain obscure and forgotten, but that together make up a chorus of witness. These are the acts that make up the church.

The politics of the church is not headquartered in Washington, DC. How many of us who feel we have all the right opinions and voted for the right person—and like to broadcast both on our bumper stickers—nonetheless struggle to turn those convictions into realities in our relationships? Here are some suggestions. Let's not complain about the American church still being segregated unless we ourselves are prepared to go and sit in a church of another tradition every few weeks to listen, learn, share, and enjoy. Let's not lament the reality of segregated neighborhoods unless we ourselves are prepared to welcome at our table and maybe offer our spare room to someone of a different history from our own. Racial reconciliation isn't something that any of us can delegate to anyone else. It's something we each have to embark on for ourselves. For a long while we've spoken the language of rights, access, and entitlement. That's important, but it can't achieve the change that really matters. It's only when the language of rights, access, and entitlement is transformed into the realities of understanding, friendship, and trust that the dividing wall of racism really begins to come tumbling down.

What matters most today is that the phrase "so that Barack could run" is not the end of the sentence—or anything like the end of the sentence. The sentence didn't begin with Rosa. It stretches back over decades and centuries of people who believed and knew that the God who had made their oppressors in God's image had made *them* in God's image too. And the sentence won't end with Barack, because sitting on his library shelf in the Oval Office will be that same dictionary as you and I both have, the one that says "black" commonly represents evil, darkness, bad luck, crime, condemnation, chaos, and death; whereas "white" commonly represents purity, peace, fairness, life, and good. Rosa, Martin, and Barack will always have honored places in that sentence. But the sentence is really about every forgotten person who lived with hatred and discrimination and responded with courage and hope. The sentence is really about those who didn't think the curse of racism in this country was someone else's problem to sort out. The sentence is really about those who lived not to themselves only but who became temples of the Holy Spirit that opened the eyes of others to the glory of God.

There's even a place in that sentence for you and me, if only we have the courage and hope to take it up.

# 17

# Can We Talk?

Imagine your life as a huge flat canvas. Colorless, empty. Dull as ditchwater. Then start playing with it. Put in some undulations, mountains—hard to cross but with great views from the top. Put in some rivers and seas—dangerous but nourishing and full of adventure. Put in some light and shade that give shape to the day. Put in some dampness and dry areas that give seasonal texture. Add some life—some beautiful creatures and some mysterious beings. Now you have a world. Put in some obstacles you don't yet know quite what to do with. Add some features that look threatening but might turn out to be humorous after all. Now you have a story. How are you going to overcome the obstacles while enjoying the beauty? How are you going to meet the beautiful creatures and find a way to live with the mysterious beings? Now you have a life.

Life as a Christian isn't all slamming down winning baskets, taking forty-yard touchdown passes, turning around to receive standing ovations, and fighting off the autograph hunters. Life as the church isn't a blank, unchallenging canvas. Things go wrong. People fall out. You get cross. You feel let down and misrepresented. People get hurt. That's not a sign that Christianity is a mistake or the church is wicked. It's a sign that the church is real. Being a Christian is not a security blanket. It's not about making sure nothing goes wrong. Something always *does* go wrong. The key is what happens when it does. The key is about allowing our weaknesses to be turned into God's opportunities. This is exactly what Matthew 18 is about.

The first thing Jesus says is, "If another member of the church sins against you . . ." (Matt. 18:15). The word *if* can also be translated *when*. In other words, Jesus says sin is going to happen. It's not a surprise, and it's not the end of the world. You will come to the office refrigerator and find that someone's taken that fantastic last piece of cheesecake you'd saved for dessert. You'll return to the parking lot and find your precious new car has a twelve-inch scratch on the passenger door. You'll check out a new apartment and find that the landlord has raised the price after you thought you had an agreement. Your old roommate will come to visit and use a word about people of another race that's widely regarded as deeply insulting. It happens. Much worse things happen.

*When* it happens, Jesus tells us what to do. "If another member of the church sins against you, go and point out the fault when the two of you are alone. If the member listens to you, you have regained that one" (Matt. 18:15). Don't try to ignore it, because you'll just build up a volcano of frustration that will erupt in the wrong place at the wrong time. Find the right moment. Don't mouth off to anyone else about it. Just say to the person, "Can we talk?" And if they say yes, just say, "Do you mind not using those kinds of words to talk about people?" Practice it, if necessary. Say it out loud: "Can we talk?" Remember, anticipation is everything. Anticipate that things are going to go wrong and you'll get better at finding the right words when they do.

Remember that Jesus in Matthew 18 has just been pleading with his disciples to become as humble as children. He's been reminding them that God longs to bring the lost back home, like a shepherd searching tirelessly for a stray sheep. In this humble, compassionate spirit, try out these kinds of phrases: "I don't know if you realized, but whenever you talk about your husband there's always a sense of complaint or criticism. I think it's maybe supposed to sound funny, but I guess it leaves me wondering if you two are really okay." "I find it difficult that you always say 'I know' whenever I make an observation. I come away feeling like I've got nothing interesting to say." Practice on these little confrontations and you'll be better prepared for the big ones.

Jesus is saying, what you're trying to do is *persuade* your brother or sister, not humiliate them. Don't see this confrontation as a disaster, a last resort, but as a moment of truth backed up by love. Think about how you want the conversation to end. Not with the other person saying, "I now realize how totally right you were and how completely wrong I was"—that's humiliation. That's preserving the fantasy of your own perpetual righteousness. Think about how to get to words like "I appreciate that. I can see what you're saying. I'll need to think some more about it . . . thank you." That's friendship.

Of course, you may fail. Your brother may not listen to you, or may take offense and blame you, or may deny there's any problem and make you feel stupid for raising it, or may accept there's a problem but then do nothing about it. That's the point at which the situation has got bigger than just you and your brother or sister. That's the moment, says Jesus, that it's time to bring in others. Jesus goes on, "But if you are not listened to, take one or two others along with you, so that every word may be confirmed by the evidence of two or three witnesses" (Matt. 18:16). These others may end up showing you it was you who was mistaken. Or they may help to persuade your friend.

If these others fail, it may be necessary to move to a third stage. This means bringing in people who don't know the parties involved directly. Jesus says, "If the member refuses to listen to them, tell it to the church" (Matt. 18:17). But remember, the whole point is not to win, not to humiliate, but to persuade, to move from face-to-face confrontation to side-by-side collaboration. It's about getting to the place where both parties are able to say thank you. And if all that fails, says Jesus, there is a fourth stage. "If the member refuses to listen even to the church, let such a one be to you as a Gentile and a tax collector" (Matt. 18:17). That doesn't mean that you never speak to them again. It means that either their faith or their lifestyle is so far from the truth that you see them as needing more than persuasion—they need *conversion*. And conversion is often a slow process that may best be facilitated by someone other than you.

Jesus concludes by saying three things that put these interpersonal interactions in a larger context. "Whatever you bind on earth will be bound in heaven, and whatever you loose on earth will be loosed in heaven" (Matt. 18:18). In other words, these confrontations, little or trivial as they may seem, really matter. They matter because they're crucial to building character, crucial to saving our souls, and crucial to building the church. They're the mountains that turn our lives from a flat canvas into a gripping series of pinnacles and ravines. Find a way of talking about the little hurts and misunderstandings, and you'll be learning how to make a good friendship, a good marriage, a good neighborhood, a good workplace. Find a way of naming and addressing sin and resentment, and you'll be beginning to see how to relate to people who insult you, people who defraud you, people who ignore you. You'll be learning how to make an enemy into a friend. You'll be learning how to bind and loose.

Then Jesus says, "If two of you agree on earth about anything you ask, it will be done for you by my Father in heaven" (Matt. 18:19). In other words, everything is possible. This is not a zero-sum game, where either I turn out to be totally right or I realize I was a complete fool and I'm going to feel like an idiot for the rest of my life. If two people are reconciled, if one says, "Sorry, forgive me," and the other says, "Thank you, I do forgive you," and the first says, "Thank you too, I never realized what a burden this was until you made it clear to me and now I feel I have gained a friend"—if you learn to anticipate and practice and expect these kinds of conversations, then there is no limit to what God can do for you. God can forgive. God can give you strength to forgive. God can give you the time you need. God can give you words to say. God can give you friends to support you, make you laugh, distract you, tease you, hug you. God can give you everything you need.

Just reflect for a moment how much energy is pent up by our reluctance to have these conversations. I imagine everyone here knows what it's like to drive to Alabama with the hovering question, "Why are we doing this, Mom?" when Mom knows perfectly well the answer is "Because Dad desperately needs to have a face-to-face conversation with your grandmother and he can't bear it so he's dragging us along to ensure we'll all be so busy he won't have to have the conversation." People move away because they can't face having the conversation they need to have with their next-door neighbor. People go to business school because they can't bear to tell their father that they really long to go to theater school. People join the army because it's the only way to get away from having to continue living in deafening silence with their younger brother.

And then finally Jesus says, "Where two or three are gathered in my name, I am there among them" (Matt. 18:20). Jesus doesn't just give us friends to help us over the mountains and across the rivers of life. He gives us himself. He is the tunnel through the unclimbable mountain. He is the bridge across the uncrossable river. He makes the woman whose son had been murdered meet, confront, befriend, and finally adopt the boy who murdered her son. He makes a man whose wife had an affair seek out and come to love the man he had once cursed and hated. He makes an African American civil rights leader befriend a man who had led the Ku Klux Klan. Such stories can take several years of pain and tears. They depend on God's strength, way beyond the strength of the parties involved. And each depends on one person finding the courage to say, "Can we talk?" Where two or three deeply want to find forgiveness and reconciliation, want to meet God in one another and find an extraordinary friend, but cannot find the strength or the courage or the words or the way, Jesus says, "I am there among them. This is what I lived for: this is what I died for. This may take years. But this is what I am all about. I am there."

So what's stopping us? Why do we try to suppress conflict like a cartoon bruise, only to find it coming up somewhere else? Because we want to be nice. I think in North Carolina there's a term for it: *southern civility*. We don't want to say, "Can we talk?" because we fear we may lose a friend. But were they such a good friend anyway, if we couldn't talk to them? We don't want to say, "Can we talk?" because we fear we may have totally misunderstood and we'll find it's actually us who's sinned against them. Well, isn't that a good reason to talk? We don't want to say, "Can we talk?" because we don't want to seem judgmental—but how often do we end up complaining to someone else and making it worse rather than sorting it out with the person themself? We don't want to say, "Can we talk?" because we think it's wisest to leave it to the lawyers—but then we live as frightened strangers in the world the lawyers create for us. We don't want to say "Can we talk?" because we're frightened that the other person may be angry or upset and we'd rather live life on a flat clean canvas than be real.

116

So why do we say "Can we talk?" Because that's what God says to us. God could have said, "I'll turn a blind eye to humanity gone astray." God could have bad-mouthed us to anyone who'd listen, or kept out of our way, or just been coolly civil while everyone pretended life was supposed to be a rose garden. But God didn't create a flat canvas. God created a world of undulations and pinnacles and crevices, a world of dry places and fertile crescents, a world of beauty and danger. God loved us. So God said, "Can we talk?" In Abraham, God took us to one side. In Moses, God had a quiet word. Most of all, in Jesus God came face-to-face with us and found words to say uncomfortable things. But God didn't humiliate us. God came in yearning humility and in compassionate kindness. True to form, we got angry, we got defensive, and we even got violent. God knows all about the cost of saying, "Can we talk?" The cost was the cross. That's how much God wanted to be reconciled with us, gentiles and tax collectors that we are. Jesus is God saying, "Can we talk?"

The question that remains open is, will we find the grace to say to God, "Thank you: you've shown me the truth. I realize now that you've been a true friend to me. I'm sorry I was so blind for so long"? Can we respond to God like that? Can we become God's friends again? And can we hear the voice of God inviting us, the loving arms of God stretched out to us, every time someone says to us, "Can we talk?"

# 18

# Can We Still
# Call God "Father"?

I once went to have dinner with some friends who lived and
worked in a youth center. The youth center board meeting was
going on the same evening in an adjoining room. When the meeting broke up, a board member appeared in my friends' kitchen with
a trolley of china coffee cups and cookie plates. One of my friends
looked half playfully, half combatively at the man who'd appeared
with the trolley. "I guess you were hoping we were going to wash
those up for you," she said. "Oh—I'm sorry," said the man, with a
plaintive look that suggested he knew he was already committed to
an explanation that was only going to make things worse. "I didn't
mean to put you out. It's just that we used to have some women on
the board and they used to do the dishes after our meetings."

Those were the days. Those still are the days in some quarters.
That man was dimly aware that the world he'd grown up in was
changing. He knew he was way out of his depth in the new world
he was entering. If you're being charitable, you say his attitudes are
dumb but harmless. You're likely to call him a dinosaur. If you're
being less charitable, you say he's determined to preserve power

in the hands of men and keep women in servile roles. You say he's part of a pervasive social malaise. You're likely to accuse him of chauvinism or patriarchy. The reason I still think about this man so many years after that evening is that he lived in a cocooned world in which there was nothing that made him think or feel he was saying anything inappropriate.

And that's the real point. For him, we all have our station in life. Men belong at the top. Whether that's because of strength, intelligence, habit, or divine decree is seldom quite clear. From this point of view, to call God our Father comes out of the same set of assumptions. The Father God puts a divine stamp on a patriarchal human package. And that's why calling God our "Father" today has become so problematic. It seems both to endorse and legitimize a world in which men run the show and women clean up afterward.

Before we look at whether we can still call God "Father," I want to pause and recognize the grief for many of leaving that old world behind. For all its shortcomings, it offered a security that many are finding it hard now to live without. Every young woman who goes to college knows that her role is to excel. She's to pursue an outstanding career, have an enviable social life, produce a trophy family, maintain a magnificent figure, and achieve a perfect work–life balance. Anyone who questions this is an enemy of freedom, and anyone who believes it may represent just a new set of burdens for women is likely to be accused of endorsing the old patriarchal package. Meanwhile many men feel paralyzed and anxious in a new world where, whatever efforts they make to equalize the burdens of life, it's somehow never enough. The suspicion always lingers that they'd gladly welcome back the patriarchal package should it ever become socially acceptable again. And that suspicion may in many cases be well founded.

On a good day this brave new world is one of uninhibited fulfill-ment and dreamlike mutuality. On a bad day it turns relationships into simmering cauldrons of pent-up resentment interrupted periodi-cally by explosions of defeated exasperation. For some it feels like they've gained freedom, but on the way lost quite a bit of the joy.

I believe the question of whether we can still call God "Father" belongs in this context of bewilderment and confusion over male and female roles in the new world that has come to pass in the last

119

fifty years. Take the proposal to change the words "Father, Son, and Holy Ghost" to "Creator, Redeemer, and Sustainer." It sounds like a way of making God more wholesome, a way of focusing on the action of God rather than getting bogged down in God's identity. It may be a recognition that the language of "Father" is painful for some, especially perhaps those who've been physically, sexually, or emotionally hurt by someone they had every reason to trust. These motivations are perfectly genuine. There's no doubt that for some the word *father* in itself is a serious obstacle to faith. But it's very hard indeed to keep the conversation about God and not let talking about language for God become simply an exalted way of talking about ourselves. Anyone who stands up for the language of "God the Father" risks being accused of wanting to restore the whole patriarchal package. The conversation about the identity of God quickly opens up profound anxieties about negotiating the new set of male and female roles available to us.

Reclaiming the feminine language of God is an important project. Jesus really does describe himself as a mother hen. Several times in the Bible we read the vivid language of "womb," "breasts," and "labor pains" as attributes of God. We need to ensure this feminine scriptural imagery is visible in the way we talk about God—not just because the patriarchal language has some troubling resonances, but also because this imagery gives us a richer understanding of who God is. The church has been very slow to recognize these things.

But if the real issue is that men have so often been violent, abusive, and domineering, we should come right out and say it rather than diverting it into a conversation about God. Maybe the fundamental issue isn't about changing the language of "our heavenly Father." It's about changing the lives of our earthly fathers. The problem isn't so much the way God is Father. The problem is the way *I'm* a father. It's time for men to become the kinds of fathers that God is. If they all were, the question of what to call God wouldn't go away, but I'm not sure it would seem quite as urgent as it does right now.

The joy of Christianity is that we've been made in God's image. But the danger of Christianity is that we're constantly tempted to recast God in our own image. This isn't a new problem. In every generation Christians have been inclined to portray God along the lines of what seemed good and right and true in the society of their time.

It's perfectly natural for us to articulate the highest ideals of what today we aspire to and then project those onto God. But it's obvious what's wrong with this approach. It makes God into a product of our creative imaginations. We become the creator and God becomes the creature. We turn into divine editors, going through every aspect of God's script, correcting it for errors; or we turn into divine professional trainers, toning up the parts of God's body we deem to be out of shape. God becomes a show pony for our own high ideals.

So the question becomes, Do we relegate the language of "God the Father" to one image among many, and a suspicious one at that, because of its associations with the patriarchal package of male dominance and female subservience? Or is there still something vital about the language of "Father" that transcends the patriarchal package and we need to keep at the center of our faith, even if some of us find that a real struggle? I want to dwell briefly on two themes.

First, when Jesus says "Abba" (the Aramaic word for "father" or "daddy"), he doesn't mean a seventies Swedish pop group, but he doesn't mean *father* in our conventional sense either. If you've ever had the privilege of putting a child to bed, seeing their trusting eyes, bending down your ear, and hearing the child whisper a question of utter existential urgency, you'll have a sense of what the word means. "Daddy, is tomorrow forever?" This is a profound, intimate, and nonsexual relationship, one of joy, trust, frustration, misunderstanding, endurance, touch, warmth, tears, and love. You don't get much of that in the word *Creator*. "Creator" is a job title. Granted, you don't get a lot of job postings with that precise title. It's a big job and it's hard to get the salary level right. "Creator" isn't fundamentally about relationship. It might evoke awe and admiration, but not love. What calling God "Father" really means is that the inner life of God is always a relationship, always an intimate, trusting, dynamic exchange, and so when in the miracle of grace you and I are invited to be in relationship with God we're invited to join a relationship that's already going on. We may be able to find other words, but whatever they are they need to express this central truth. God loves passionately and intimately, but nonexclusively, and the words we use need to convey this.

The second theme that affirms God as Father means getting away from the idea that the father is the only one who really matters.

121

I have a theory that in most families there's one strong character and nothing really functions unless that person's happy. Everything is organized to ensure that that person gets their sleep, food, and TV-watching on cue, as if they were a baby. I once played a game in a friend's house where everyone present was asked the question, who's the strongest character in this household? and everyone there said it was the eldest child, who happened not to be there that day. We then had a brief but poignant moment of recognition that the whole household existed to make that one person happy. The Trinity isn't like that. It's not a hierarchy, and the Son and the Holy Spirit aren't going around treading on eggshells in case the Father loses his temper.

When I was in high school I wanted to be the center of attention. I wanted to be an actor. In my first year at college I got a part in a play. It wasn't a play that changed the face of modern drama. But it changed me. Almost every line was funny, and for the first time I realized that I didn't have to get all the laughs. For the first time I got as much joy out of setting up the other players for the funny lines. For the first time I discovered that performing wasn't a competition for the audience's scarce attention but a reveling in one another's gifts and interpretations.

The Trinity isn't a support structure for the Father to be the star. It's a circle in which each member is relishing the joy and the challenge of bringing the best out of one another. Hierarchies can be useful if and when they enable a group of people to relax for a while and know who does what and not get in each other's way. Our station in life is a role we take on for a limited period to get a job done as a team. Once you make a hierarchy more than that—once you start saying our station in life is a fixed part of our identity—it's a disaster. The Trinity isn't a fixed hierarchy. It's more like a company of actors who take different roles depending on the play they're performing. God is always in an inner relationship with God's own self and at the same time in an outer relationship with us. So the circumstances are always changing. The fun and the drama are always to discover how things will turn out this time. And in case we think this is turning into a fantasy summer camp from the sixties, of peace, freedom, cupcakes, and crumbly candy bars, let's never forget that the cross seared the heart of God the Father and the Holy Spirit and not just the Son, and so at the heart of this mutually indwelling love is the reality of sacrifice.

So we've seen that God is fundamentally about nonexclusive relationship and nonhierarchical flourishing. There's nothing in the doctrine of the Trinity that underwrites the patriarchal package we continue to be so anxious about. The curious thing is that when we put the constructive characteristics of God the Father on the table we see that if we're going to hold on to gender stereotypes, God's characteristics often sound more stereotypically female than male. God is compassionate and merciful (Exod. 34:6; Pss. 86:15, 103:8, 116:5; Isa. 30:18); in Hebrew, the word for "compassion" is closely related to the word for "womb."[1] God loves and yearns for and is fiercely protective of God's people just as a mother (Jer. 31:20) and, in fact, even more than a human mother ("Can a mother forget the baby at her breast and have no compassion on the child she has borne? Though she may forget, I will not forget you!" [Isa. 49:15]). In light of this, for most of the history of the church it's been women rather than men who've best reflected the first person of the Trinity, by demonstrating just this kind of compassion, mercy, tenderness, and fierce protectiveness of the weak or wounded.

Now this is incredibly challenging for all of us. It means God is not a father in any stereotypical human way. It means when we speak of the First Person of the Trinity as "Father" we may have to put aside most of the usual resonances of that term, the bad ones and the good ones.

We could say that this is just silly, that our gender stereotypes and bad associations aren't going to go away, so why not just coin another term? What's the point of using the term *Father* if God the Father is so very different from most human fathers? There's really only one simple reason: *Father* is the word Jesus used. *Father* is the word the Second Person of the Trinity used to speak to the First Person.

The Old Testament hardly ever calls God "Father." Maybe a dozen times, if that. But in Jesus we get something we'd never seen before. We get a window into the inner-trinitarian conversation. Jesus

---

1. H. Simian-Yofre, "*rḥm*," in *Theological Dictionary of the Old Testament*, vol. 13, ed. G. Johannes Botterweck, Helmer Ringgren, and Heinz-Joseph Fabry; trans. David E. Green (Grand Rapids: Eerdmans, 2004), 437–52; T. Kronholm, "*reḥem*," in ibid., 454–59.

addresses God as Father not once or twice but maybe 170 times. This is the most intimate, most loving, most precious, most vital relationship in the whole universe and beyond, and we've been allowed a window into it. Isn't that window a most incredible privilege?

And it turns out it's not just a window. Romans 8 tells us that through the Holy Spirit we've been invited into this most intimate and dynamic of all relationships. Paul writes, "For you did not receive a spirit of slavery to fall back into fear, but you have received a spirit of adoption. When we cry, 'Abba! Father!' it is that very Spirit bearing witness with our spirit that we are children of God, and if children, then heirs, heirs of God and joint heirs with Christ—if, in fact, we suffer with him so that we may also be glorified with him" (Rom. 8:15–17). We've been drawn by adoption into the loving embrace of the Trinity. We're going to dance to the end of love. This is the most astonishing miracle of all. It's the miracle we rediscover every time we remember Jesus invited us to say "Our Father" when he taught us how to pray. Not just his Father—*our* Father.

This is a gift beyond price. Jesus is inviting us into his own experience of life within the Trinity. In saying the Lord's Prayer we are being invited to see what God is like from the inside. That's what these precious words mean—that there's a relationship at the heart of all things and by the miracle of grace we've been invited into it. The language of "God the Father" isn't shoehorning all of us, whatever our personal histories and whatever ways God has been revealed to us, into a one-size-fits-all, take-it-or-leave-it form of prayer. To say "Father" isn't to express our *own* experience of God. We can do that in a hundred ways, female, male, and beyond. Our own experience of God is important, but it's not what finally saves us. Our own intimate and diverse experiences of God are not what the language of "Father" is finally about. The point is, to say "Father" is to celebrate that we've been drawn into *Jesus's* experience of being part of the Trinity. And it's *that* experience, rather than our own, that saves us.

# 19

# Casualties of Destiny

Lord Mountbatten was the last viceroy of India under the British Raj. He had many opportunities to observe Mahatma Gandhi's ascetic lifestyle and commitment to simplicity despite his demanding political role. It is reputed that when Mountbatten commented on Gandhi's lifestyle to Sarojini Naidu, one of Gandhi's close aids, Naidu retorted, "You'd never guess how many people it takes and how much it costs to keep that man in poverty."[1]

You could say the same about Abraham. Abraham's story is like a grand superhighway. It begins with his call from God and the blessing that came with it, and then the promise of a son for his wife Sarah. But in other parts of the story we can see the soil that is turned up to make that superhighway, the cost of keeping that man in his blessing, the number of people it takes to keep him as a great patriarch. In Genesis 21 we see Abraham as the car driver who says, "I never have road accidents; but I see a good many in my rearview mirror."

In Genesis 16 and 21 we read Hagar's story. Reading Hagar's story is like looking over the minority report of the Old Testament. It's also like peeling an onion. Each layer you take off makes you cry

---

1. This possibly apocryphal quotation is variously attributed to Naidu, to Lord Mountbatten, and even to Gandhi himself in the 1982 film *Gandhi*.

harder. I'm going to start with an outline of her story and then peel down two or three more layers to see what we find.

God promised Abraham he would be the father of a great nation. But his wife Sarah was old and childless. We peel off the first layer of the onion when we see that Sarah and Abraham couldn't see a way for God's promise to be fulfilled, so they took matters into their own hands. Sarah suggested Abraham sleep with her Egyptian slave girl Hagar and get an heir that way. Hagar conceived and straightaway began to look down on her mistress, Sarah. Sarah complained to Abraham, and Abraham said, "Do what you like," so Sarah was cruel to Hagar, and Hagar ran away. An angel of the Lord met Hagar in the wilderness and told her to return and submit to Sarah and look forward to having a great many descendants. Hagar called the Lord El-roi, or the "God of Seeing," and in due course she had a son named Ishmael. Later, much to the surprise of Abraham and Sarah, Sarah had a son Isaac—but Sarah once again demanded that Abraham throw Hagar and Ishmael out. God backed Sarah up but also promised that Ishmael would become the father of a great nation. Abraham packed Hagar off to the wilderness with meager provisions, which duly ran out; Hagar placed her son under a bush and wept to watch him die. Feel the tears take effect when you hear Hagar say, "Do not let me look on the death of the child" (Gen. 21:16). But God heard the boy's distress, and called to Hagar, and she saw a well of water. Ishmael grew up in the wilderness, and Hagar eventually went and found a wife for him from Egypt. That's the story of Hagar.

Now let's look at the story a little more closely and peel off another layer of the onion. Hagar's story is Israel's story. She's a slave, just as the children of Israel later became slaves under the Pharaoh. Just as Israel became a threat to Pharaoh when Israel grew in number, Hagar becomes a threat when she has a son. Just as Israel ran away from bondage in Egypt, so Hagar runs away from the cruelty of her mistress. And just as Moses met God in the wilderness, so Hagar meets God in the wilderness. Just as God promises Abraham that Israel will become a great nation, so God tells Hagar that Ishmael will also be a great nation. Hagar's story is Israel's story—but there's a crucial difference. When God tells Hagar she will have many descendants, the prophecy is not accompanied by any promise, or any blessing. It's just a stark foretelling. There's no guarantee that God will be on Hagar's side.

If the first definitive moment in Israel's story was the exodus, then the second definitive moment is the exile. Just as Hagar is like Israel in running away from slavery and having her own exodus, so later she's like Israel in being thrown into exile. Like Israel, Hagar knows both exodus and exile. And just as it is for Israel, exile for Hagar is an agonizing and purifying time. She and her son survive, and adapt, and meet God there too, just as Israel did in Babylon. And yet, again, God seems not to be on Hagar's side. As one Bible scholar puts it, Hagar "experiences exodus without liberation, revelation without salvation, wilderness without covenant, wanderings without land, promise without fulfillment, and unmerited exile without return."[2]

But it's not just in exodus and exile that Hagar mirrors Israel's story. Genesis 21 and Genesis 22 sit side by side with one another. They're obviously meant to be read together. In Genesis 22, God tells Abraham to take his son Isaac and sacrifice him on Mount Moriah. At the last minute God intervenes and provides a ram instead. In Genesis 21, God allows Abraham to follow Sarah's wishes and cast Hagar and her son out into the wilderness, where Ishmael is on the point of death when God intervenes and provides water. Over and over again we are being told that Hagar's story is Israel's story. And yet there's this constant irony and paradox that Hagar is the person steamrollered to make Israel's story possible. It's as if Israel looked into a puddle and saw reflected back the face of Hagar.

It's time to take another layer off the onion and prepare to cry a little more. The story of Hagar and Sarah is the story of Arab and Jew. Possibly the most distressing line in the whole story comes when Sarah sees her son Isaac and Hagar's son Ishmael playing together and she can't bear it. If ever there were a description of the sins of the parents being visited on the children, surely this is it. Isaac and Ishmael are set at odds against one another because Sarah couldn't abide any comparison or comradeship between her son and Hagar's. But again at this point the interpretation of the story is soaked in irony. The force behind the establishment of the State of Israel is that the Jews of history have felt less like Sarah and more like Hagar.

2. Phyllis Trible, *Texts of Terror* (Philadelphia: Fortress, 1984), 28.

It is because they've been thrown into slavery, subjected to cruelty, forced to flee, and frequently cast out that they came to long for a home to call their own; and it is because in the middle of the last century they sat powerless, like Hagar, watching their offspring die, that they came to see a homeland as an unmitigated necessity and its preservation as an absolute good that continues to justify a number of things that are less than good.

The paradox of the Middle East today is that both sides think they're Hagar and meanwhile act like Sarah. The sense of grievance in the Muslim Middle East today arises because so many Muslims perceive that the mantle of Abraham has passed to America. Rightly or wrongly, few Muslims in the Middle East see themselves as the Abraham about to cast out the Hagar that is the State of Israel. Instead many Muslims in the Middle East see themselves as the Hagar, ill-used and cast aside by the feckless Abraham that they regard as the United States, aided, agitated, and goaded by the jealous Sarah that is the State of Israel. Yet again this story comes back to haunt the self-styled children of destiny. Much of the Muslim world says, "America doesn't have any road accidents—but we are the casualties America sees in its rearview mirror." Muslims tend to identify with Hagar, seeing America as Abraham and Israel as Sarah. Sure, Hagar provoked Sarah something rotten, but Hagar had by far the worse end of the deal. And the tragedy is that the children of Hagar and the children of Sarah don't get to play very much together. If they did, they might forget their parents don't get along.

What are we to do about this disturbing story, this story that shakes us out of any simple notions of God's call, God's promises, and God's faithfulness, and leaves us crying as if we had been peeling an onion?

This story is an education in human complexity. No one comes out of it terribly well. We feel sorry for Sarah, dragged halfway across the Middle East in pursuit of a destiny revealed to her husband but never properly to her. There's a good number of people who know exactly what that feels like. Sarah is childless, and that for many people is an agonizing condition. But when Sarah uses her slave woman for her own purposes and then blames the slave woman for the consequences of what were, in fact, her mistress's decisions, we lose sympathy for her. We feel very sorry for Hagar, but be careful before we turn this

into a goodies and baddies story. Note that it was when she humiliated Sarah that Hagar's fortunes took a downturn. Some of us may
sympathize with Abraham, wringing his hands as the women in his
life outmaneuver him. Others may regard him as weak and lacking
authority or any sense of justice. As for God, it's not clear whether
God has it in for Hagar or simply allows Abraham and Sarah to face
the consequences of their own lack of faith. Who among us hasn't
doubted God's promises? Who among us hasn't turned our head from
injustice and simply wanted not to look? Who among us hasn't said
"Yes!" in a vindictive way when "Yes!" really meant getting one up
on someone who has often been mean or cruel to us? Who among us
hasn't blamed God for situations we really got ourselves into?

So to read this story is to realize that salvation is not a simple
story of progress from wilderness to destiny. It's a whole lot more
human than that. Every character in the story is deeply flawed—just
like you and me. Even the description of God offered here is pretty
uncomfortable. It's very common to see Genesis 22, the story of
Abraham almost sacrificing Isaac, as a troubling story, because it
seems to portray a God who wants distressing things from us. But
it could be that this story from Genesis 21 is an even more troubling
story, because it seems to portray a God who not only lets people
suffer but actually prefers some people to others. In our desire to
celebrate Abraham it would be very easy to miss the troubling attitude
of God to Hagar. And it would be easy to overlook our tendency
to identify with Sarah, the one who bought her freedom at terrible
cost to another child of God.

Why, then, is this story in the Bible? If the story of Abraham was
a simple march to destiny, you'd think this story would have been
left out. If it really is the winners who write the history, why would
they bother to waste time on the losers, especially the losers they
treated so badly?

Maybe those who looked back on Israel's history realized who
Hagar really was. That's why the story notes that she's the first
person in Scripture to be visited by an angel and the only person
in Scripture to give God a name—El-roi, the Seeing God. She's the
only woman to receive God's promise of descendants. She is the first
woman to weep over a dying child. So she's a pretty special woman
in many significant ways.

But we still have to struggle with why God seems to reject her. And for Christians the fact that God seems to reject her has to be the key to this story. Think about it. This is a person who was in the midst of the story of God's covenant. This is a person who embodied Israel's exodus and Israel's exile. This is a person whose suffering seemed to be required if Israel was to live. Yet this is a person whose suffering was exacerbated and even brought about by the character flaws in those who were God's chosen people. This was a person who was cast out and, in her moment of deepest agony, wondered why her God, her God, had forsaken her. This was a person who was despised, rejected, and acquainted with grief. Sound familiar? *This* is why the story of Hagar is in the Bible. Because her story, the story of exodus, exile, and rejection by woman, man, and even God, is the story of Jesus.

For Christians, the story is in the Bible to make sure we remember that Jesus looks more like Hagar than he does like Abraham. For Christians, the story of Hagar means that there can be no freedom, no good news, no salvation, no gospel that's won by treading down, expelling, abusing, and exploiting Hagar. But there's not an ounce of sentimentality in this story. At the very beginning, we're told that Hagar is no angel. The point is not that Jesus identified with the honest but with the browbeaten, oppressed peoples of the earth. The point is that Jesus is to be found among those who may well have contributed to their own downfall but are, in all likelihood, more sinned against than sinning, and either way are to be found today wandering, weeping, scorned, and rejected.

It's a complicated story, with intense feelings, laced with cruelty, betrayal, terror, and despair. It's complicated, but in the light of the gospel it's actually quite simple. We have a pretty good sense of which kinds of people in which kinds of places read this story and instinctively identify not with Sarah, not with Abraham, but with Hagar. You may feel it's hard to see Jesus, hard to feel close to him, hard to know he is truly alive. Hagar's tale is a story in which one person seems to have to suffer so that God's people may flourish. We all know people who are on the underside of life, on the underside of history, who find themselves in car wrecks in the rearview mirror of destiny. You may feel like you're looking for Jesus. Maybe, in meeting Hagar, we just found out where to find him.

# 20

# The Three Realities of AIDS

In 1982 the Centers for Disease Control, based in Atlanta, first coined the term *Acquired Immune Deficiency Syndrome*. The term described the collection of symptoms and infections resulting from the specific damage to the immune system caused by the human immunodeficiency virus (HIV). Since then, twenty-five million people have died of the disease, making it one of the most destructive epidemics in recorded history. It's currently killing people, around one-sixth of them children, at a rate of three million per year. Without antiretroviral drugs the average length of time between contracting HIV and developing AIDS is about nine years, and the life expectancy after developing AIDS is around nine months. The attention of the media for anything that develops slowly is always difficult to sustain, and some researchers have found that in the developed world media coverage of HIV/AIDS has declined dramatically over the last 20 years.[1] But it's the most deadly disease of our time.

In the early 1990s one of my favorite TV programs was called *Dinosaurs*. It was a bit like *The Simpsons*, in that it took social

1. Publications Office of the European Union, "Media coverage on AIDS pandemic shrinks, study finds," CORDIS News, December 12, 2010, http://cordis.europa.eu/fetch? CALLER=NEWSLINK_EN_C&RCN=32821&ACTION=D.

issues and parodied them in a domestic setting. In this case it was a family of dinosaurs. One running joke was that the dinosaur family would gather around their own television to watch their favorite show. The show was called *Way Too Complicated*. Whenever a dinosaur wandered into the sitting room and said, "What are you all watching?" the answer would be "It's *Way Too Complicated*." And that's what I want to address here. What do we do with a global epidemic whose causes and dimensions and casualties feel just way too complicated? What difference does AIDS make to our faith, to our discipleship, to our lives?

For many of us, in the face of sickness, suffering, and a staggering level of global distress, there's a strong urge simply to turn away. We want to turn away because we want to protect ourselves from being overwhelmed. After all, our own lives are not so invulnerable, and we spend most (or all) of our days trying to make some order out of the chaotic world around us or the fragile world inside us. To turn and face an ocean of suffering is like allowing ourselves to be engulfed in a tidal wave of grief, and our instinct for self-preservation pulls us away from the danger of drowning. To see suffering is to recognize that this suffering involves me. We're not especially proud of turning away, and we may be generous in sending money to address the problems we fear to look at; but one way or another we know that seeing reality for what it is will be too much for us. So we look away.

There are subtle ways of looking away that don't involve just turning the head. While searching for cures in laboratories and research clinics is urgent and necessary, simply to concentrate on AIDS as a scientific issue can be to turn one's face away from the sheer human reality and dynamics of the disease. Perhaps a more common refuge is the resort to moralizing. Few other diseases have been subject to such a torrent of judgmental speculation and condemnation. Knee-jerk, armchair moralizing is essentially another way of not seeing, of protecting ourselves by not facing, naming, focusing on, and sitting still in the presence of enormous suffering. If only we could say that people somehow *deserved* this illness, that they had caused their own downfall, then somehow we could shield ourselves from the horror of it all. But it's seldom as simple as that, and even if it were, when someone is hurting as badly as this we have to ask ourselves why our reaction is icy condemnation rather than loving compassion.

The reason is that compassion means seeing. And we fear that if we truly see we will be overwhelmed. Our carefully guarded cordon of safety will be invaded. So what can we do to stop ourselves from looking away? There's a kind of seeing that asks God to give us strength to gaze at things that cause us pain and threaten to overwhelm us, things we would rather pretend were not there. The name for that kind of seeing is *lament*. We find a great deal of this lament in the Old Testament, particularly in those passages that mourn the loss of Jerusalem and the going into exile—in the books of Lamentations, Jeremiah, and Psalms. In poetry, singing, simple music, silence, taking refuge in one another, the beauty and gentleness of God's purposes, and the final destiny of his creation, we find the strength to see the truth about the world and dare to wonder at the truth about God. If we are to live with AIDS, we have to learn to see the human cost of AIDS; and to see AIDS, we have to learn to lament.

But to see AIDS also means to see the world. And much of what causes AIDS and is wrong with the world was wrong well before AIDS came along. Our self-protection makes us call AIDS a sexual disease, a disease there would be less of if there were less casual sex. This is self-protection because it presupposes everyone in the world lives in a world of rational choices made from locations of significant personal independence. A world like the rich world, in other words—or at least a world like the rich world shorn of our visceral and sometimes destructive longings and desires. But that is not the world everyone lives in. The vast majority of people living with AIDS live in a very different world. This very different world is a world of poverty and gender inequality. (Not that our world is without poverty and gender inequality. But this is on a different scale.) Identifying at-risk behavior means a very different thing in social conditions where life is cheap and thus all behavior is at-risk behavior. Washing changes its meaning in a situation where the water is so contaminated that you don't know whether using it makes you cleaner or dirtier. Sex should always be about tenderness, about trust, about mutually expressing and embodying God's profound desire for us; but in such circumstances of poverty and powerlessness, can anyone be surprised that sex becomes a means of oblivion or an instrument of domination? And of course the principal casualties of such conditions are women and children. It's estimated that for at least 30 percent of young women in sub-Saharan Africa their first sexual experience is nonconsensual. In the face of such statistics, one has to *see*, to *face* the world disclosed through the lens of AIDS. Of course sexual assault is a reality in our own culture, perhaps even in our own lives. All the more reason, then, to be prepared to see a very unjust world and not turn our heads aside. Perhaps the real ways to address AIDS are to give villages access to clean water, to strengthen education, especially for women, and to strengthen economies in such a way as to make the sex trade comparatively less lucrative. In other words, the best way to stop people from dying of AIDS is simply to give them more to live for.

And when we *have* seen the reality of AIDS and the reality of those living with AIDS, and when we have seen the realities of the world that AIDS discloses, then we must see one further reality: the reality of God. AIDS is such a painful and demanding catastrophe that it forces us to search deep within the heart of God. And what I believe we find is Jesus himself. We find that in his incarnation, particularly in Bethlehem, Jesus identified with the homeless, the refugee, the child of uncertain parentage, the politically oppressed, and thus with the poor of the earth. There is no one who can fall so low in the degradation of their life and not at that very moment turn to one side and see Jesus lying in the gutter beside them. That is close to the essence of what the incarnation means. It means we are never alone, whether our pain and isolation are caused by others or by ourselves. And then in his ministry Jesus gathered around him those who lived lives of shame, disease, and exile in the society of his day—especially those with culturally embarrassing ailments and those associated with sex in ways that were considered shameful. It was precisely because these were the people he called his companions, because these were the people he touched and embraced and ate with, that he was rejected by polite society. So already Jesus tells us a lot about AIDS. But there's more.

When Jesus died he was practically naked. He died the most shameful death his era had dreamt up. He died with disreputable people on either side of him, and his friends couldn't deal with the fear, the shame, and the humiliation. But in his death Christians have seen an amazing exchange. His blood is somehow exchanged for our blood. He takes our diseased, distressed, failing blood into his own body, and in return he fills our body with his very lifeblood, blood that transforms, blood that supplies, blood that never runs out. You could call it a kind of divine blood transfusion. The very moment that causes most panic to those of us who believe AIDS cannot touch us, the blood transfusion, is in a sense a sacrament of the very transformation that Christ's death on the cross brings about for our salvation. In so many ways the imagery and metaphor of the AIDS epidemic takes us to the heart of God in the crucified Christ. This is our hope: that God in Christ takes our blood into himself and gives us his own blood that we might ever live with him.

And then in Jesus's resurrection we see God's destiny for a world restored. We see that sin doesn't have the last word. We see that suffering, of ourselves and of others, doesn't have the last word. AIDS doesn't have the last word. The last word is Jesus's restored (but still scarred) body; the last word is our own bodies, scarred but restored, as his companions forever. That is our hope: that the God who came among us in Christ, stood with us, took our sickness and death into his own body, and transfused us with his lifeblood, will come again. And we shall be God's companions forever.

These are the three realities of AIDS: the personal, human reality of fear and suffering; the global, social reality of poverty and gender inequality; the divine, incarnate reality of transfused passion. Only when we have seen all three of these realities, only *then* is it time to respond. Only then is it time to speak and act in the face of AIDS. Only when we have seen the human reality of AIDS, and lamented. Only when we have seen the global reality of AIDS, and named the issues of power and poverty at the heart of it. Only when we have seen the reality of God, and worshiped the transfusing Christ who has identified with us, taken us into himself, suffered with us, and overcome death for us. Only then is it time to respond.

And how *do* we respond? Our response has the same three dimensions as the shape of our seeing. We respond personally, preferably by befriending someone with HIV or at least by coming to know a person working regularly with these people and these issues. The best thing Princess Diana ever did was to touch a person with AIDS. Maybe the best thing we could do would be to do what she did. We respond structurally, by avoiding sentimentality and directing our energies and resources toward programs that genuinely address the poverty and powerlessness that make such fertile ground for this disease. If we don't want people to act in ways that put their lives at risk we have to give them more to live for. And we respond spiritually, by recognizing that an encounter with this disease is an encounter with God, and that our faithful engagement with it may change others but will certainly change ourselves. Personally, structurally, spiritually: this is how we respond. And we can't respond alone, or else we will certainly drown in despair. We respond together, through the personal, structural, spiritual body of people that we call the church—the human, social, and divine body of Christ.

You'll have realized that in most of what I've said here I'm not talking just about HIV or AIDS. I've been talking about how we live as Christians and as the church in the face of troubling issues and global problems—issues and problems that most of the time just seem way too complicated. What I'm commending to you is a spirituality and an ethic of seeing and responding. It's about patiently seeing, not rushing to moralize or diagnose. It's about seeing a second time, seeing underlying causes and global realities. It's about seeing a third time, seeing the heart of God in the coming and passion and trans-fusion of Jesus. And only then is it about responding—personally, structurally, spiritually. This is what it means to live as the body of Christ—even when the body of Christ has AIDS.

# 21

# He Is Our Peace

The twentieth century gave us some striking examples of what it means to be at peace: 1919; 1945; 1969.

At the Versailles Conference in 1919 the Allied powers decided peace meant defeating Germany and then keeping it in a straitjacket for as long as possible. Peace meant punishment and constant policing. At Hiroshima and Nagasaki in 1945 peace meant killing two hundred thousand people at a stroke. Peace meant destroying and intimidating to a sufficient degree to end war, and then making sure your enemy didn't get hold of the wherewithal to do the same to you. At the Woodstock Festival in 1969 peace meant smoking pot, growing your hair down to the ground, and driving a rainbow-colored VW Beetle, and doing all three while making love to anyone you could get your hands on.

These are the kinds of images that come into our minds when we hear the word *peace*. Such a diverse range of uses makes the word *peace* seem either vague and idealistic or cynical and manipulative. The New Testament is neither vague nor idealistic nor cynical nor manipulative. It has two words for peace. One of those words is *Jesus*. Ephesians 2 gives us perhaps the most concise description of the way Jesus is peace. Here are the five ways that Jesus is peace. All of them center on the word *one*.

First, Jesus makes *one new humanity*. It says he "has broken down the dividing wall, that is, the hostility between us. He has abolished the law with its commandments and ordinances, so that he might create in himself one new humanity in place of the two [i.e., Jews and gentiles], thus making peace, and might reconcile both groups to God in one body through the cross, thus putting to death that hostility through it" (Eph. 2:14b–16). I want to take a moment to explain why Christianity steers a unique path in political thought. One of the most significant questions in modern philosophy is, Are humans all fundamentally the same, or are we different from one another in ways that aggregate us into separate and competing groups? There are two conventional answers to this question.

One says we are all fundamentally the same. This is the bumper sticker that proclaims, "One race—the human race." The assumption seems to be that if we all realize we're the same we'll all suddenly be at peace with one another. The more we ignore or eradicate our differences, the happier life will be. We could call this the sophisticated version of the Woodstock approach. The trouble is, once we suppress our differences, we become unrecognizable to ourselves, let alone to one another. Peace becomes a form of denial.

The other conventional answer to whether we're fundamentally the same or different says, no, we really are all different, and asserting our identity is central to our being, even though those differences—of age, mobility, intellect, genes, wealth, race, gender, access to resources, and so on—make conflict with one another a perpetual and probable danger. So we need nation-states, regulated government, and careful policing to prevent us from killing one another. This is how we got to Versailles. The trouble is, it's also how we got to Nagasaki. Peace becomes an olive branch covering the nakedness of raw power.

But Christianity says to both of these answers, "Why do you assume that difference leads to violence? Why do you assume that violence is more basic than peace? Yes, we are all different from one another, but in God's sight difference is made for peace. Difference creates beauty, creativity, flavor, color, texture, harmony. Violent conflict lurks among the shadows of difference and sometimes breaks into the foreground, but antagonism isn't written into the DNA of difference. God made us to be different from one another because he had a myriad of different things he wanted each one of us to do. We aren't made in a factory to be identical widgets; we are made by an act of love to rejoice in the detail of our difference from one another. The fundamental difference is the difference between us created beings and God the Creator, and it's in the tension and creativity of that difference that life resides. Harmonious difference is what the universe is all about."

Think about someone you're struggling with right now. You're probably bewildered or infuriated by their difference from you. But there's no use ignoring the difference, and you can't control their effect on you forever. The only answer is to find a way to make that difference creative and constructive. That may feel like a daunting prospect. But it's the only prospect you can genuinely call peace. Ephesians says Jesus brings us that peace. But it was daunting for him too. The cost to Jesus is the blood of his cross.

Jesus doesn't abolish difference. He's the embodiment of harmonious difference. He brings God and humanity together. He brings Jew and gentile together. He makes possible, demonstrates, and renews a world in which Technicolor diversity can flourish while each entity enriches the life of every other. That's the kingdom of God. That's what his life, death, and resurrection give us, now and forever.

So Jesus transforms our fears about being different. And the second thing Jesus does is to transform our fears about being the same. Jesus makes us, in verse 16, *one body*. When we read the words "And the Word became flesh" (John 1:14), we recall how Jesus became a human being like us. He brought divinity into our humanity. But just as significant is what Jesus did in the other direction. He brought humanity into the heart of God. When we say Christians are the body of Christ, we're not just saying that there is a divine dimension to everything Christians do together. We're also saying that the joy, the blessing, the struggle, the sin, and the pain of human striving on earth are taken up into the life of God. This is the paradox of Christian belief: God is utterly *different* from us—eternal where we are temporal, all-knowing where we are foolish, all-loving where we are self-absorbed. But God is unbreakably *connected* to us through Jesus in a way that does not diminish God but only ennobles and enriches us. The image Ephesians gives us of what it means to be both different and the same is the picture of one body, with countless interdependent parts. "So then you are no longer strangers and aliens, but you are citizens with the saints and also members of the household of God, built upon the foundation of the apostles and prophets, with Christ Jesus himself as the cornerstone. In him the whole structure is joined together and grows into a holy temple in the Lord; in whom you also are built together spiritually into a dwelling place for God" (2:19–22). To demonstrate how much that is at the center of God's purpose and identity, in Ephesians that body is called Christ's body (5:30).

I wonder what your greatest fear is. For most people it is being finally fundamentally alone. The fear of pain and death is only a part of the bigger feeling of being utterly alone forever. And the most destructive things people do tend to arise out of a terror that they are or may become utterly alone. Jesus's gift of peace to us is to promise that he will never leave us alone.

So this is how these first two priceless gifts fit together. We are *different* from one another, and in Christ that difference from one another becomes part of the dynamism of our difference from God, and so it leads not to endemic antagonism but to kaleidoscopic creativity. But yet we are *one body*, and in Christ that means we are deeply bonded to one another as we are deeply bonded to God. That is what peace means.

And the third thing we discover, this time in verse 18, is that we have access to the Father in *one Spirit*. The Holy Spirit is the part of God that gives us here and now and forever and always those things that Jesus brought us once and for all. Jesus has shown us and brought us peace, but we need the Spirit to continue to make peace in and among us. The one Spirit proclaims "peace to you who were far off and peace to those who were near" (2:17). One of the most difficult things in life is to balance your care for those who are near—your regular circle of friends, family, neighbors, and colleagues—with your responsibility for those who are far off—distant friends, family, fellow citizens, and people of other nations and faiths. In Charles Dickens's novel *Bleak House* he describes one Mrs. Jellyby, who spends every hour of the day campaigning about the plight of the people of faraway Borrioboola-Gha while failing to see that her own neglected children are disintegrating around her. We all know how easy it is to become so wrapped up with a small circle of intimates that we can't register the needs of those outside our own tiny world. I don't think I know anyone who really gets this balance right, however hard we try.

It's hard to be at peace with those who are far and at peace with those who are near. In Ephesians those who were far off are the gentiles and those who were near are the Jews. But it's just as easy to think of those who are far off as meaning those who feel by their life and actions they've put themselves beyond the reach of God and those who are near as meaning those who feel they're just the most righteous and worthy people of all time. I wonder whether you're more at peace with those who are far off, or with those who are near. I wonder whether you feel you've put yourself beyond God's mercy, or whether you feel you're "nearer to God than thee."[1] Jesus is our peace because he gives us the Holy Spirit to reconcile those from whom we are far off and those to whom we are near. Jesus is our peace because he gives us the Holy Spirit to reconcile the parts of ourselves that are far from God with the parts of ourselves that are near.

The fourth thing Jesus makes, in verse 19, is *one household*. "So then you are no longer strangers and aliens, but you are citizens with the saints and also members of the household of God." The three Greek letters *oik*, which represent the core of the word for "home," appear no less than six times in the last four verses of Ephesians 2—we have "aliens," "household members," "built," "structure," "built together," and "dwelling place," all coming out of the same root of "home"—*oik*. And the same root gives us the words *economics* and *ecology*. And it's economics and ecology that show us the full significance of how Jesus brings us peace.

How does Jesus transform economics and ecology? Think for a moment about what both disciplines take for granted: that there's not enough. Economics says there's not enough money, not enough wealth, not enough health care, education, GDP, equity, liquidity—whatever there is, there's not enough of it. Ecology says there's not enough oxygen, ozone, species diversity, rain forest—you name it, there's not enough of it. Economics and ecology are all about scarcity. And so of course they presuppose conflict, because we're bound to fight over limited and diminishing resources.

But Jesus is all about abundance. The resurrection of Jesus proclaims that there's more than enough of the things that last forever. There's more than enough life in everlasting life; there's more than

1. "Nearer, My God, to Thee" is a nineteenth-century hymn by Sarah Flower Adams.

enough mercy in the forgiveness of sins; there's more than enough joy in the song of heaven; there's more than enough love in the peace that passes all understanding. Jesus's economics and Jesus's ecology bring us peace because they teach us the secret of happiness, which is learning to love the things that God gives us in plenty and that never run out. Things like love, joy, and peace. Jesus doesn't give us too much of the things we fight over, because we'd still fight over them. Instead he gives us in plenty the things we don't need to fight over. We call these things the words of eternal life. That's how Jesus is our peace.

And the fifth thing Jesus makes, in verse 21, is *one holy temple, one dwelling place for God*. This is the climax of the whole symphony. Remember, step one was, we think difference makes conflict, but in Christ difference makes kaleidoscopic creativity. Step two was, we think we're alone and isolated, but Jesus bonds us unbreakably with one another and with God. Step three was, we think we're bound to tread on and fight with those close to us, or club together with those close to us to fight those who are far away, but Jesus gives us one Spirit that reconciles us to those near and far. Step four was, we think we live in an economy of scarcity, but Jesus creates an ecology of abundance. The more we keep assuming conflict is unavoidable, the more Jesus shows himself to be our peace.

Finally, he makes us into one temple. That means he makes us the place of encounter with those who long to meet and be reconciled with God. He turns us from his huge problem into his simple prayer. He transforms us from a battleground to a sanctuary. He makes us the living example of his salvation. He makes us the embodiment of peace. Finally, after the greatest battle of them all—the one Christ fought for us on the cross against sin, death, and the devil—he makes us into a peace the world has never before known, and everything becomes worship. That's what heaven is—the place of harmonious diversity where we as one body, whether saints who know we've had a past or sinners who know we have a future, enjoy the things that never run out and all finally becomes worship.

As I said earlier, the New Testament has two words for peace. The first one is Jesus. I didn't say what the second one is. There is a second one. It's what happens when there is harmonious difference, costly unity, constant reconciliation, never-failing abundance, and everything finally becomes worship. The second word for peace in the New Testament is *church*.

# be not afraid of faith

Believers fight other believers over a shade of difference. Doubters fight only with themselves.[1] Yet it's easy to fall into avoiding the details of faith, for a number of reasons. One can feel faith is such a scarce commodity that one shouldn't be too picky about its particulars. One can be anxious about alienating those with strong views about particular doctrines, and seek peace by avoiding controversial subjects. One can be so anxious to urge disciples to moral righteousness or social action that one has little time to linger on the whys and wherefores. One can be wary of sounding pious, or reluctant to commit oneself to a conviction one may later come to doubt. Or one can find the gap between Scripture and theology too wide, and the theoretical steps between them too obscure, to feel confident about stepping into sophisticated territory. In short, expressing faith may be hard because faith is scarce; but it may also be hard because faith is deep, and things deeply held can be hard to put into words. These are among the reasons disciples may avoid talking to one another about faith.

1. "The believer will fight another believer over a shade of difference; the doubter fights only with himself." These lines are from Graham Greene's novel *Monsignor Quixote* (New York: Simon and Schuster, 1982), 55.

Yet we all thrive on encouragement. We all thirst for others to offer us compliments, attention, or a sense of common enthusiasm or humor. When Christians share their deepest truths together, those truths are not all fearful. Some truths are ones of tentative, growing, or articulate faith. But it's possible, indeed too easy, to establish a culture in which sharing doubt and distress is acceptable but sharing hope or consolation is not. Disciples need to create spaces and opportunities where gleanings may be cherished together, encouragement may be offered, and appropriate challenge may be articulated.

To do so requires compassion, vulnerability, and patience. But it also requires passion, humor, and confidence. These are the qualities the following reflections seek to show.

# 22

# Time to Shed the Cloak

Some years ago I got a surprise visit from a man I hardly knew. He was the chief executive of a prominent corporation in the city in which I lived. He was one of those people who, however wealthy or senior he was, could never succeed in looking tidy. Somehow the hair, shoes, or beard always looked a bit out of control. I'd only met him once before, and even then we'd only spoken for a few minutes. He sat in the corner of my study, chewing his fingernails and rather nervously holding a homemade cassette. (For those who don't know, audio cassettes were things we used for recording music in days gone by, after the era of long-playing records and before the time of compact discs, which themselves were back in the days before we gave up listening to music because the skill required to master the technology was greater than the pleasure gained by hearing the song.)

I hazarded a guess that small talk wasn't what my visitor had come for. He broke the ice. "I've come to see you because there's no one else I can tell. I want to be a Christian. In my world that's like saying I'm crazy. I expect you know that. Last night I got up in the early hours and made this tape and it says what I want to say and I want to leave it with you because there's no one else I can give it to." I think he became a Christian the moment he gave me that tape.

Sometimes it's as simple as that. Of course there were probably years of wrestling and who knows how many sleepless nights spent pacing around at home. But in the end, he just drove to find the only pastor he knew, handed over the tape, and that was that.

Looking back, I think that moment all those years ago was the closest I've come to meeting Bartimaeus. Short as his story is, Bartimaeus is one of the most significant characters in the Gospels. Mark's Gospel is divided into two halves. The first half is set in Galilee. Jesus heals people and calls disciples, and in between times he teaches, often in parables, and gets into trouble with the authorities. In the second half the scene shifts to Jerusalem. There Jesus faces controversy, his identity is disclosed, and he's led to crucifixion. The story of Bartimaeus is the climax of the first half of the story.

To understand it, you need to go back to the parable of the sower in Mark 4. You'll remember that Jesus talks there about four kinds of earth: the path, the rocky ground, the thistles, and the good soil. The first half of Mark's Gospel illustrates these four kinds of discipleship. Some seed falls on the path: this refers to the authorities that reject Jesus outright, the scribes and the Pharisees. Some seed falls on the stony ground: this refers to the disciples, especially Peter, James, and John, who accept the word immediately but wither in the face of temptation or persecution. Some seed falls among thorns: these include King Herod, who takes to Jesus but is mired in a network of unsavory commitments, and the rich young man whom Jesus calls but who just can't leave his money behind. And then there's the good soil. This refers to those who hear and accept the word and bear fruit in abundance. There aren't a lot of these in the Gospels. But Bartimaeus is certainly one of them. Mark's Gospel tells a story in which those who are the professional holy people, those who have most exposure to Jesus and his teaching, and those who have the most money and status, all fall away and are all supplanted by this solitary blind beggar, who alone does exactly what Jesus wants—he "followed him on the way" (Mark 10:52). Thus the first becomes last, and the last, the blind beggar Bartimaeus, becomes first.

The heart of the story of Bartimaeus lies in his cloak. The cloak is the one thing he has. It's his source of protection from dust, wind, rain, and cold. And it's his source of income, like a street musician's open guitar case. This is the crisis of the story: Bartimaeus *has* one

146

thing and he *wants* one thing. He *has* a cloak and he *wants* to see. How much does he want to see? Enough to part with his cloak? Absolutely. He leaps to his feet and hurls away his cloak. He parts with the one thing he has in order to receive the one thing that really matters. And Jesus stands still, as if to emphasize the timelessness of this moment, and asks Bartimaeus the penetrating question, "What do you want me to do for you?" Bartimaeus has no hesitation. He knows *exactly* what to say: "My teacher, let me see again" (Mark 10:51).

The rest of the first half of Mark gives us plenty of examples of people who, unlike Bartimaeus, can't bring themselves to shed their cloak. People like us. This story confronts us with two overwhelming questions: Are we prepared to shed our cloak? And, when we come face-to-face with Jesus, do we know what to say?

How fervently we organize our lives in order never to be in Bartimaeus's position! Isn't this what our accumulation of wealth and possessions is all about? Wealth and possessions are the best and most resilient kind of cloak we know. They protect us from the vulnerability of facing personal, medical, career, or social disaster. The trouble is, the more we possess, the more our possessions possess us. Managing money, managing property, and managing our public image is time-consuming to the point of becoming overwhelming. We become like the Michelin Man, surrounded by layers of insulation, and the idea of springing to our feet and following Jesus seems impossible. And when Jesus says, "What do you want me to do for you?" our first instinct is almost bound to be a request to firm up the insulation. "Errr . . . it would be handy if you could raise house prices again, please."

But wealth and possessions are by no means the only cloak in the closet. As we see in James and John, status is just as compelling. What is status really, and why do we crave it? Status is a way of trying to assure ourselves that we have everyone's admiration so we can convince ourselves we don't need their love. That's what the chief executive who paid me the surprise visit was struggling with. He was coming to terms with the reality that he was going to lose people's admiration and was going to need their love in a way he'd never had to ask for it before. If we won't allow ourselves to shed the cloak of status, and Jesus asks us, "What do you want me to do for you?" what will we say? Something like, "Make everyone admire me or envy me or at least fear me, but never put me in a position where I need them to love me."

Scholarship is its own kind of cloak. It's a cloak of knowledge. It doesn't matter whether it's philosophy, medicine, theology, or aeronautical engineering, when we've read all the primary literature, and all the secondary literature, and every single scholarly article on a subject, we've built up a pretty impressive cloak. We know all there is to know. We can think of a thousand reasons not to leap to our feet and a hundred ways to deconstruct Jesus's call. But where does that get us in facing Jesus's question, "What do you want me to do for you?" The answer isn't in a book. What are we going to say? "Make me a bigger library"?

And before we get too pious and get to thinking cloaks are some kind of worldly thing, let's not forget there are plenty of religious cloaks too. Maybe we've had a profound religious experience or two. Maybe we're so determined to focus on the significance of our own experience that it becomes our cloak, the thing we can't part with when Jesus calls us. Maybe we're anxious that other Christians seem to be a bit fuzzy on matters of Scripture or ethics or whatever we've tried long and hard to be so certain about. Our certainty, our religious orthodoxy and righteousness—that too can become our cloak, so that when we stand face-to-face with Jesus and he says, "What do you want me to do for you?" all we have to say is, "I sure hope you're going to live up to my very precise expectations." Just imagine if Jesus turned out to be less correct than us.

We may have made for ourselves a cloak of social righteousness, where we've managed to boycott all the right things, avoid eating all the wrong things, correct everyone when we catch them using insensitive or inappropriate language, and know exactly what kind of footprint we're leaving on precisely which part of the ozone layer. What will we say to Jesus when he asks, "What do you want me to do for you?" Will we find ourselves saying, "With all due respect, Jesus, it's time you changed the car you drive"?

We're all different and we all have different challenges and different temptations. But here's one last cloak I think maybe a lot of us have. It's the tendency to think of the Christian faith as some kind of life insurance package, which doesn't require a great deal of us in our lifetime other than a verbal assent and a monthly or biweekly deduction from our paycheck. It needs a bit of adjustment when there's a major family-life transition, like a wedding or a funeral, but otherwise it just ticks over like a useful but unobtrusive insurance policy, lifting anxiety about the future and making it easier to plan for the unknown. We live in a corporate world, and we're used to delegating the complex parts of our lives to the professionals: how convenient to get God to handle the eternal life contract. When Jesus says to us, "What do you want me to do for you?" we'll just say, "Give me what I've paid good money for."

If we remotely recognize ourselves in any of these descriptions, or if family, nation, or anything else has become our cloak, the story of Bartimaeus is saying one simple thing to us: it's time to shed the cloak. Making such a cloak for ourselves amid the uncertainty of life and the fear of death is understandable. Keeping such a cloak as our source of identity and security is a very common thing to do. But if we truly want to meet Jesus face-to-face, if we long to leap up in delight and joy because we've put our trust in no one and nothing but him, *it's time to shed the cloak.*

Imagine Jesus calling you from the other side of a fast-flowing river. You're wearing the cloak, your precious, carefully customized cloak. He's calling you by name and you start to cross the water, still wearing the cloak. You go deeper and deeper, and the cloak is getting heavier and heavier, and anyone watching could see that if you don't shed the cloak it's not just that you won't see Jesus, you won't even make land on either bank. I wonder whether that's where you are.

It's time to shed the cloak. It's time to part with the insulation, to dispense with the insurance package that prevents you from coming face-to-face with Jesus. The rich young man wouldn't part with his money. That was his cloak. James and John wouldn't part with their longing for status. That was theirs. It's time to shed the cloak. God shed the cloak by coming naked among us in a manger in Bethlehem, by hanging naked before us on a cross outside Jerusalem. God shed the cloak because God wanted so desperately to stand before us. It's time for us to shed ours, so we can stand before God. It's time to shed the cloak.

Why must we shed the cloak? Because Jesus is going to ask us, "What do you want me to do for you?" And if we're all bound up

149

in the cloak we're going to be very limited indeed in the range of answers we're going to be able to give him. In particular, we're going to find it impossible to give the answer Jesus wants to hear. We're not going to leap up in joy like the blind beggar; we're going to find ourselves dreading the conversation.

When Jesus asks, "What do you want me to do for you?" Bartimaeus simply says, "Let me see again." Think about what these words really mean. Bartimaeus is saying to Jesus, "I want you to change my identity." Bartimaeus is blind, and he's a beggar. That's what he is and how he makes a living. When he begins to see he loses his identity as a blind man. He loses his security of income as a needy person whom others feel obligated to help. He's stepping into the unknown, a world he can't begin to imagine.

Small wonder we don't want to shed the cloak. Because then we'd be stepping into the unknown. We'd find ourselves standing before Jesus and saying what Bartimaeus said. "I want you to give me a new identity. I want to become what only you can make me. I want to open my eyes and enter a whole new reality—like a blind man opening his eyes to see the world for the first time. Let me into that world. Please, Jesus! Please, Jesus: I'm leaving my cloak behind. I realize now it's useless. Let me into your world!"

After the chief executive left my house all those years ago, I found myself with an audio cassette in my hand. I made my way to the tape player and slotted it in. I heard on the tape the sound of my visitor clearing his throat, in a rather self-conscious way. Then there was a long silence. Then he cleared his throat again. And then to my astonishment I heard this proud man begin to sing a simple song. "I have decided . . . to follow Jesus. I have decided . . . to follow Jesus. I have decided . . . to follow Jesus. No turning back. No turning back."

# 23

# Born Again

My father was the kind of person who, if he found something funny, would find the same thing funnier the second time, and even funnier each time he repeated the joke. One of my happiest memories of our life together is of late evenings when I had a French test the next morning. He would help me practice my French verb conjugations, especially the irregular ones. There were two verb forms he tested me on repeatedly, and they never ceased to tickle him because he couldn't imagine when anyone would ever be in a position to use them. Of course I remember them to this day. One was the perfect tense of the verb to die—*je suis mort*—"I have died." The other was the future tense of the verb to be born—*je naîtrai*—"I will be born."

I will be born. Fancy being in a position to say that. It's an undoubted fact that far and away the most stressful experience any one of us has in our lives occurs over the minutes or hours or even days that follow our mother's water breaking. Putting it in simple terms, it's mighty cozy in the womb, it ain't easy getting out, and your skull gets bashed about so much that its bones have to remain soft until after the short but momentous journey is all over. It's not surprising that most babies come out screaming their heads off and wanting their money back. In fact, if a working definition of freedom is that you're never made to do anything you haven't agreed to do and you get the maximum physical and emotional comfort level the maximum amount of the time, then being born rightly qualifies as the worst experience of our lives. It's possible some of us never get over it.

In John 3 Jesus meets Nicodemus, a leading scholar and teacher of his day, and Jesus says to him, "No one can see the kingdom of God unless they are born again" (John 3:3 NIV).[1] On the face of it, it's hard to see how that can be good news. As we've just been recalling, being born is a complete nightmare: no light, confined spaces, pain, coercion, the unknown—it's straight out of a horror movie. And Jesus is saying we've got to do it all over again. If that's the good news, what, we may ask, is the bad news? Nicodemus, however, is not a man especially in touch with his feelings. He's not thinking about the psychology; he's thinking about the biology and the physics. "How can anyone be born after having grown old? Can one enter a second time into the mother's womb and be born?" he says (John 3:4). In other words, "But grown-ups are too big to fit back in. How does it work? Could you just draw that for me?" "Oh no," says Jesus. "It's not just a trick of getting a big clumsy genie back into a little tiny bottle; this is about a wholesale transformation—body, mind, and spirit. It's going to make the first birth look like a picnic." Nicodemus then turns into a cartoon character whose eyes expand and rotate like the dials of a slot machine.

The most curious thing about this whole exchange is that this one verse of John's Gospel, which contains enormous mystery, wonder, and, to say the least, lack of clarity, has become arguably the single most important verse in the American church. I say that because around 40 percent of Americans describe themselves as born-again Christians. The phrase "born again" makes a lot of people, Christian and non-Christian alike, feel uncomfortable, I think for a number of reasons.

In the first place it's become associated in the last thirty years with a particular political agenda and a set of conservative stances on controversial social issues such as abortion and gay marriage. It's hard to believe these issues were at the front of Jesus's mind when he struck up a conversation with Nicodemus, but such issues certainly seem to be in the minds of those who see being born again as being

1. The NRSV renders it, "No one can see the kingdom of God without being born from above." The word translated "from above" can also mean "again."

a member of a political block vote. My sense is that this view is at best a caricature, and that many of those who describe themselves as born again have a diverse set of perspectives on social issues. But there's no doubt it's a caricature with a wide circulation.

In the second place the term *born again* seems to be used to create a hierarchy among Christians. In certain circles it is not considered good enough to believe in Christ, to be actively involved in the church, to be seeking to grow in faith, and to practice discipleship by searching out and standing among the people and issues closest to God's heart—all these are looked down upon unless one can narrate a conversion experience that fulfills the description "born again." The result is that many Christians much of the time feel pretty second-rate because they know that faith is a matter of God's grace, can't be manufactured, and so they can't make themselves have a dramatic experience. Yet God seems to have no interest in giving them one. Again, this is an exaggerated picture, but there's enough truth in it to shape many Christians' lives significantly.

In the third place the experience of being born again seems to displace everything else that's important about Christianity. What matters is not who Jesus is or how Jesus lived, nor how Christians relate to one another in the church, to the neighbor, or to the stranger in the world. All that matters is *my* personal experience on a specific day in the past and *my* certainty that this experience gives me a passport to heaven when I die. In other words, Christianity stops being about Jesus, the church, and the new world breaking in and instead becomes all about *me*. This describes a general tendency rather than a universal reality, but again there's enough in the tendency to attract a lot of reservations.

That's a brief summary of why the term *born again* is the elephant in the room whenever the church reads John 3. This legacy is a terrible shame, not only because it tends to discredit some of the most faithful Christians in this country, but because the term *born again* could and perhaps should be integral to the whole church's understanding of itself. Let me explain why.

In *The Republic* Plato describes the experience of being in a deep cave, one that slopes downward at an angle.[2] Near the bottom of the cave is a group of people. The people are facing the back wall of the

2. Plato, *The Republic*, bk. 7.

153

cave at its deepest point. Above and behind them, nearer the cave entrance, is a fire, which provides all the light in the cave. Between the people's backs and the fire is a puppeteer. The puppeteer moves around puppets depicting animals, plants, and other things; and these shadow images are reflected on the back wall, which becomes like a cinema screen. This is the only reality the people in the cave know.

Now, suppose one of the people down in the cave were to get up—or to be picked up and carried. Either way, suppose that person somehow made their way all the way up to the entrance of the cave. Three things would almost immediately happen to them. First of all, they'd be practically blinded by the overwhelming light, having always previously lived with next to no light at all. Second, they'd be overwhelmed to discover that the reality of the world outside the cave far exceeded the reality inside the cave by any imaginable measure. And third, they would instantly and painfully begin the process of re-narrating the history of their own lives and the nature of reality in the light of this wholesale new experience of the way things really are.

I want to suggest to you that becoming a Christian is like coming out of that cave. It's not necessarily a sudden thing, because it's possible to see the light while still remaining far down in the cave and it's possible to linger at any point on the way, especially at the entrance of the cave, and it's even possible to go back into the cave if the world outside is just too much, too scary, or too wonderful to take in. It's not primarily about your own efforts, because you can be carried up to the entrance of the cave, and you'd probably never know the entrance was there unless someone came down and told you. It's not necessarily a judgment on people of other faiths or none, because the important thing is not to obsess too much on the benightedness of the cave and the importance of getting out of it. The point is to concentrate on what it's like to live outside of that cave. And that's what Jesus does with Nicodemus, a man who appears pretty keen to stick to the cave he knows, and pretty reluctant to be brought out of it. Notice that he comes to Jesus by night (John 3:2).

Jesus tells Nicodemus, "This is what it's like to live in the wondrous and dazzling new world outside the cave"—otherwise known as "the kingdom of God." Jesus starts by saying that it's a world of "water and Spirit" (John 3:5). This makes us think of baptism—which for many, perhaps most, Christians is exactly what being "born again"

154

means. But I think in this context water means the ordinary and Spirit means the extraordinary. So Jesus is saying the wondrous new life includes the divine but it continues to include the very mundane. Water means life, and Spirit means eternal life. Water means our full humanity, our neediness, our doubt, our hopes, our love. And Spirit means God's full divinity, searching for us, transforming us, shaping God's life to love us. And of course Jesus is the place where water and Spirit, humanity and divinity, meet.

Next Jesus says, "The wind blows where it chooses" (John 3:8). It's always worth remembering that *wind* and *spirit* are the same word in both Greek and Hebrew. The only real problem with the familiar language of being "born again" is if it suggests God has only one way of operating. But here we're told that the wind blows where it wills, that the Spirit isn't subject to conventional limitations and always retains an aura of mystery. Don't live in a smaller world than God has given you. If the cave was a kind of prison, don't turn this new world into a new prison. The amazing world outside the cave is a world where God's activity is limitless.

Last and most significantly, Jesus talks about being "lifted up." He says, "And just as Moses lifted up the serpent in the wilderness, so must the Son of Man be lifted up, that whoever believes in him may have eternal life" (John 3:14–15). The fabulous life outside the cave involves being lifted up. But in the background we know that for Jesus being lifted up didn't just mean the resurrection and ascension. It meant being lifted up on the cross. The world outside the cave is a fantastic one, but we are lifted into it through the lifting up of Jesus's cross. Leaving the cave is not without cost, pain, or trauma, but the heat of that transformation is borne for us by Jesus.

So we discover the qualities of the dazzling new life outside the cave by studying the life of Jesus. In Jesus we see God's divinity most fully revealed through our full humanity. In Jesus we see the limitless potential of the Holy Spirit. And in Jesus we see that God's purpose is to lift us up, to lift us out of the cave, and so we imitate Christ most closely when we are lifting others up—lifting others out of the cave. When Jesus is asked to describe the kingdom of God, he describes his own incarnation, ministry, and resurrection. Jesus is the shape of the dazzling new life we've been given.

And these insights should indicate what's missing from the conventional caricature of being born again. The conventional caricature is simply way too limited. In the first place Jesus is about a whole lot more than creating a political machine to manipulate American elections. In the second place the Spirit has much more than one manner of helping us out of the cave and into dazzling new life. And in the third place God is a great deal less bothered about our having a particular personal experience than about our lives being lifted up like Jesus's was and about us spending our lives lifting up the lives of others.

So there's more to faith than being born again. But being born again is still central to the language of faith. Because emerging from the cave is also a straightforward description of what it's like to be born. A baby moves from a small, restricted, but secure space with no light into the limitless reality of life. Being born is just like emerging from a cave. Being born is the moment in life that shows how the wondrous creative power of God is revealed through our vulnerable humanity. Being born is the moment we emerge into limitless possibility. And the moment we are born we are lifted up, by careful medical professional or overwhelmed parent. So coming to faith is just like being born.

And there's one more birth. There's one more emergence from the cave. The promise of Jesus is not just that when we live in him we shall enter limitless life, like a prisoner emerging from a cave or a baby emerging from the womb. The promise goes one stage further. It's that Jesus's tomb was also a cave. Jesus went into a cave to bring us out of the cave. When Jesus emerged from the cave that first Easter morning, he broke the shackles of our imprisoned life and offered us dazzling newness. The reality is that we shall die, and we ourselves will be placed in a cave. This isn't just about the past; it's about the future. But Nicodemus learns that Jesus was lifted up, that nothing can constrain the Spirit, and that God is most fully revealed in our most human moments. And so the promise is that, after the lightlessness, fear, and constraint of death, we shall be born again to eternal life with God. So the good news is not so much "You *must* be born again" or "*Unless* you are born again. . . ." The good news is, "You *shall* be born again, and you shall emerge from the cave of death to the light of life."

My father was right. It really is the best verb in the language. "I will be born." Again.

156

# 24

# What's Wrong with God

A month after my ordination I was called to an overcrowded house in the poorest part of town. All I knew was that a fifty-three-year-old man was dead. I knocked at the door, and a young man in his early twenties answered. He saw my clerical collar and realized straightaway I'd come to talk about his father's funeral. Without pausing for breath he said, "Most people when they have a heart attack get a second chance but my dad just dropped dead out of the blue so there isn't a God then is there?" Sensing this wasn't the moment to run through the top ten arguments for God's existence, I tried to hold his gaze. I simply said, "I'm sorry." The young man stared back at me for what seemed like minutes and finally looked down at the doormat and said, in resignation, "Why don't you come inside?"

When it comes to reasons for not believing in God, you'd think that stories like this would be well up there. Somehow in allowing this kind of suffering in the world it seems God has lost the moral argument. Meanwhile the discoveries of modern science are sometimes construed as suggesting God has lost the intellectual argument. It's easy to get ahold of some wonderful discoveries about life, the world, and the universe and project from there that everything in existence can be reduced to a bunch of mathematical formulas. And then there are other faiths. For some people the fact that so many people believe so differently is evidence that we all somehow made the whole God thing up. God has lost the moral and intellectual argument, and now seems to have lost the practical one too.

But these big three questions—suffering, science, and other faiths—seldom turn out to be the great obstacles to faith they're cracked up to be. The young man I talked to on the doorstep wasn't saying, "I've lost my faith," he was saying "I'm in tremendous pain and grief." You can't be angry at something that doesn't exist. The discoveries of science deepen our sense of wonder at God's creation. They don't require us to assume that nature is a mindless machine. The existence of other faiths tells us that most of humanity in most places for most of human existence has had some kind of faith in God. To me, those all sound more like arguments *for* God than against God. Suffering, science, and other faiths don't really have to be such big obstacles to faith.

I'll tell you what I think the *real* obstacle to faith is. It's more in the heart than the head. Jesus seems so far away. That's it. That's the problem. Jesus just seems so far away. In fact it's three problems.

Problem one is that Jesus seems far off because two thousand years seems so *long ago*. We know in our heads that in the whole history of the world two thousand years ago isn't yesterday; it's a second or two ago. We've all seen those charts that map the history of the world onto a twenty-four-hour clock. Most of the twenty-four-hour day is filled with rocks and no animate life, then the amoeba has the planet to itself for a while, before the much-maligned dinosaurs fill up a lot of the rest, and humanity emerges in the last two seconds and Jesus is born about a millisecond ago. That should make us think Jesus is very close, but it doesn't. We live lives shaped by air conditioning, retirement packages, bank accounts, and news media—and first-century Palestine is like a fairyland of donkeys, demons, sandals, swords, and a desperate lack of dentists and deodorant. It doesn't matter how many life-application Bibles we read, Jesus just comes out of another world. That's problem one: Jesus seems so *long ago*.

And here's problem two. Jesus seems far removed because he really is literally so *far away*. One of the reasons so many Christians feel drawn to go on pilgrimage to the Holy Land is because Jesus seems so close there. Jerusalem feels distressingly full of guns, politics, and postcards, but the Sea of Galilee really feels like a place the Sermon on the Mount could be preached this very day. Visiting Galilee is like a grieving parent returning to the site of a family beach holiday—every wave on the shore is an echo of Jesus, and every shimmer on the sea could be Jesus walking on the water. But Jesus being far away isn't just about geography. It's also about cosmology. Jesus is in heaven. However much we know the distance to heaven isn't measurable, like working out how far it is from here to San Diego, we can't help feeling heaven's a whole lot more than a four-day road trip. And so we feel like the grieving parent. We can hang around the places Jesus hung around, but they only make the ache of his absence more acute. That's problem two: Jesus just seems so *far away*.

And here's problem three. Jesus seems far away because he's so *different* from us. In our multicultural society we constantly talk about difference, and usually we mean race or gender, and sometimes class, religion, or sexual orientation. There's no doubt Jesus was different from most of us in race, from many of us in class and gender, and from almost all of us in religion—he *was* a Jew, after all. But the biggest difference is the one we don't mention in a multicultural world so much. He was just so darn *good*. In my pastoral experience the biggest reason people stay away from organized religion is that they know they're mean, greedy, lustful, and selfish, and they somehow get the idea that that means God's not for them. When we know we've let ourselves, others, and God down, our first instinct is to run and hide from one another and from God. Jesus may have done amazing things for us, but sometimes those amazing things just make us feel all the more how wretched we really are. That's problem three: Jesus seems so *different* from us.

Well, that's the bad news. But still we say, "We believe in the Holy Spirit." And that's very good news. Because the doctrine of the Holy Spirit is all about what Christians have discovered is God's answer to the problem that Jesus seems so far away. God doesn't deny that Jesus is far away. The good news isn't that we're mistaken about Jesus being long ago, far distant, and very different from us. The good news is that God has sent us the Holy Spirit. And the Holy Spirit offers three words that address the three problems I've just identified.

159

Word number one is *now*. Jesus feels long ago. But it's the Holy Spirit who makes Jesus present *now*. It's the Holy Spirit who gives us words when we don't know how to pray. It's the Holy Spirit who sends us angels in ordinary human form when we don't know where to turn for help. It's the Holy Spirit who makes Jesus present in the bread and wine of Holy Communion. It's the Holy Spirit who comes down in baptism and makes the believer a child of God and a part of the body of Christ. It's the Holy Spirit who comes into our ears, eyes, and hearts when we read the Bible and turns the dry words on the page into the living Word that renews, revives, and transforms. The Holy Spirit brings us the heritage of what God has done in the past, and the destiny of what God promises to do in the future, and makes them both present. That's word number one. The Holy Spirit makes Jesus present *now*.

And word number two is *here*. Jesus feels far away. But it's the Holy Spirit who makes Jesus present *here*. If we're honest, we need to recognize that for some people all of the time, and for all of us some of the time, the far-awayness of Jesus is actually a good thing. When Jesus is far away he can remain an intellectual pursuit and a theoretical option. It's only when Jesus is here that we have to face whether we're going to follow him or not, and we search around desperately for a fence to sit on, but we suddenly find every shop in town is clean out of fences. It's only when Jesus is right here that he's scary, because he wants our heart, and while he's about it he doesn't just want our heart, he wants our soul and mind and strength too. Some people go on about the heart a lot, and some people find that alienating because they're not the emotional type—and if that's you, my suggestion is, stick with the soul, mind, and strength for now, because that's plenty to be getting along with. The Holy Spirit takes Jesus from distant Palestine and faraway heaven and puts him right here. That's word number two. The Holy Spirit makes Jesus present *here*.

And word number three is *us*. Jesus feels very different from us. But it's the Holy Spirit who makes us like Jesus. It's the Holy Spirit who gives us gifts we never before had that make us rise to the occasion when God asks us to do something we thought we could never dream of. It's the Holy Spirit who nurtures us like young trees and sees fruit grow in us, sees us become patient where we'd only known

160

exasperation, sees us find peace where we'd only experienced anxiety, sees us develop gentleness where we'd only known haste and clumsiness. It's the Holy Spirit who gives us power to stand up and not be crushed, to face failure and not despair, to make friendships in spite of our fears. The technical word for all of this is *sanctification*. And the key to it is to see that word number three isn't the singular *me*; it's the plural *us*. The gifts, fruits, and power of the Holy Spirit aren't given to us privately—they're shared among the whole church. No one has all of them. If we're short of some of them, we probably haven't been hanging around each other enough. The Holy Spirit doesn't make us individually like Christ. The Holy Spirit makes us *together* like Christ. If we want to be like Christ, we have to hang around the church, hang around one another. That's word number three. The Holy Spirit makes Jesus present in *us*.

One of the wisest people I've ever met was a palliative care physician in Scotland. This is what he once said to me: "I went to visit a cancer patient in her home. She looked thin and fragile. I've never been much good at small talk, so I pointed to a photograph on the mantelpiece and tried to be cheerful. 'You've certainly got a beautiful daughter,' I said. There was a long silence. The woman gave me a look that sliced straight through me. 'That was me, six months ago,' she said. I was speechless. I just found strength to say, 'I'm sorry. I'm so sorry.'"

For me that physician shows us a lot about the Holy Spirit. When he made his colossal pastoral gaffe he could've curled up in excruciated embarrassment and run straight out the door. It was the Holy Spirit that kept him in the room. The Holy Spirit somehow gave him the grace to be *now*—to forget about his mistake and instead to focus everything in him and beyond him on a woman who needed every ounce of strength, insight, and expertise he could give. The Holy Spirit somehow gave him the power to be *here*—to leave aside the concerns of his life and be entirely present and aware of what God was doing in that room. The Holy Spirit somehow gave him the compassion to be *us*, to communicate gently and sincerely to that fragile woman that they were in this together, that he was deeply in touch with her pain. And somehow all three of those priceless qualities were perfectly expressed in the way he said those simplest of words, "I'm sorry. I'm so sorry."

I can't tell you how hard I've tried as a pastor to be able to say those words as he said them, how much I've wanted to be filled with the Holy Spirit as he was filled, how much I've yearned to help the congregations and people I've served to know the power of the Holy Spirit in those three words, *here, now, us*. If we want to be bearers of God's Holy Spirit, and we want to make Jesus present to people like that fragile woman with cancer and that young man who'd just lost his father, we need to let ourselves be shaped by the astonishing, liberating, and exhilarating news of these three simple words. *Here. Now. Us.*

We began with everything that seems to be wrong with God. Jesus is too long ago, too far away, too different from the very human disciples. But we end with the three amazing things we discover when we truly encounter the work of the Holy Spirit. God is present right now. God is at work even here. God is truly alive in us.

# 25

# I Want to Know Christ

We each know the skepticism, or the wondering, or the anxiety, or the blind terror that maybe Christianity isn't true after all. Could it possibly be that the whole Christian faith is founded on a fantasy or a fraud, a misunderstanding or a mistake? I want to suggest that we aren't the first to think such things.

When I think about these kinds of fears, I have two friends in my mind. One is a young woman who has always felt her faith was second-rate and a huge disappointment to her parents. Her parents are the kind of people who seem to be on first-name terms with Jesus. They have as little doubt about themselves as they do about him. Jesus is always placing things on their hearts; but he never seems to do so on hers. When she sits in church she feels like she does with her parents—this constant sense that God is talking to others and not to her. It's either unreal or it's unfair. So she's starting to stay away.

Another friend is a man a few years older. Faith used to fill his soul like blood fills the heart. It all made sense to him and shaped his existence. But just recently his faith seems to have been obliterated, as if his heart had been ripped out and he was struggling to get his blood round his body some other way. His friends are looking for psychological explanations, but he doesn't want one because he's already lost his present faith and some kind of psychological explanation makes him terrified he'll come to think his past profound faith was a fantasy too. And he can't bear to think that. What he had was as real as anything he'd known. It's just not there right now.

I think of these friends when I read chapter 3 of St. Paul's Letter to the Philippians and see something there that I believe gives both of them hope. Paul says, "I want to know Christ and the power of his resurrection and the sharing of his sufferings by becoming like him in his death, if somehow I may attain the resurrection from the dead" (3:10–11).

I find these words amazing. This is Paul, remember. The man who wrote part of the Bible. That's the Bible that a lot of people call the Word of God, and some even regard as infallible. And he's saying, "I want to know Christ." Not "I know all about Jesus and all about God, and take it from me, you accept this stuff or you're eternal toast." Not that at all. Instead, "I want to know Christ." Feel the tentativeness of it. "I want to know Christ." In other words, I don't yet quite know for sure.

Now maybe for some of us that tentativeness instills a level of panic. Surely, we may feel, the Bible is supposed to present to us rock-solid, unshakeable faith. Yet here is St. Paul, the most famous apostle and evangelist in Christian history, and he's saying that even he, right now, doesn't know it all. Does that make you panic? Does that mean there's never been anyone, in the whole history of the church, who's known for sure? Is that terrifying?

Or is it incredibly liberating? Does it, instead, make you think maybe faith's not about being certain? Maybe it never was. Maybe faith begins where certainty stops. If you feel you've never found faith, maybe it's because you've been mistaking faith for certainty. If you feel you've lost the faith you had, maybe this is the moment faith really begins.

"I want to know Christ." Feel the tentativeness of it. Paul was a passionate man, but he doesn't exaggerate his faith. And read that last line—". . . by becoming like him in his death, if somehow I may attain the resurrection from the dead." There it is again! Do you see it? Do you see that word *somehow*—"if *somehow* I may attain the resurrection from the dead"? He's not 100 percent sure of his

164

knowledge of Christ, and he's not 100 percent sure of what Christ has in store for him when he dies.

Now I'm not going to blame you if you find this deeply disturbing, because for a lot of Christian history this part of Paul's testimony and this dimension of Christian faith have been airbrushed out. The great revivals that shaped the church in eighteenth- and nineteenth-century America were largely founded on Jesus being a guaranteed instrument to help you bypass hell and enter eternal life. The most successful brands of Christianity are those that make Jesus a handy device for material prosperity, inner peace, spiritual adventure, or cultural dominance. But Paul is talking about something different.

Let's look at precisely what Paul tells us about Christ. He says three things.

First he says, "I want to know the power of Christ's resurrection." If Christ wasn't raised from the dead, the Christian story is a tale of doomed love in which God makes one last pathetic attempt to win our love back. It's a story that ends in agonized failure on the cross. But if Christ *is* raised from the dead, if Christ is raised . . . then God's love is *not* finally in vain, *our* love is not finally in vain. Agonizing as it often feels, all that is done for love *will* finally become fruitful. Death does *not* have the final word. Hope really *is* the shape of tomorrow. All our pain, shame, and regret *will* finally be redeemed. Nothing is finally wasted. Fear will finally pass away and joy will prevail. All will finally become beauty. That's the only power that finally matters. Financial power, military power, nuclear power—no power is finally a power to compare with this. The power of resurrection is the power that dismantles every other power. When Paul says, "I want to know Christ," he says he wants to know this power, the power of resurrection.

Then, second, Paul says, "I want to share in Christ's sufferings by becoming like him in his death." You wonder whether Paul had ever heard the phrase "Be careful what you wish for." If Jesus is a device for getting us to earthly comfort or eternal blessing, then Paul's desire to suffer is bizarre, meaningless, or misguided. But Paul is talking about love. Paul is saying, "I don't just want to be the beneficiary of Jesus's resurrection. I want to enter into the very process by which the resurrection came about. I want to go into the heart of darkness with Jesus, that I may come to discover more wonderfully the splendor of light." Think again for a moment of my friend whose previously profound faith had disintegrated recently. He knows what Paul's talking about. He would rather walk through intense suffering, even face death, provided he knew he was close to the heart of God, than face the daily superficialities of life alone.

And then, third, this tentative possibility. Paul says, "if somehow I may attain the resurrection from the dead." That *somehow* again. It's almost an afterthought. Maybe an afterthought is *exactly* what it is. Maybe this is exactly the point. Knowing Christ is knowing the power of his resurrection. If you know the power of his resurrection, of course you'll take on his sufferings and even his death. It's more than worth it. And naturally you hope to receive the blessings of eternal life after your own death. *But even if you don't it would still be worth it to know Christ and the power of his resurrection.* That's the heart of it all. Faith is precisely in this discovery: that to know Christ and the power of his resurrection is worth any suffering and is the heart of everything *whether it ends up with the gift of eternal life or not.* Yes, we hope to be given everlasting life as the gift and fruit of Christ's resurrection. But faith begins, indeed eternal life begins, the moment we let go of our own destiny and say, "I want to know Christ and the power of his resurrection *whatever the suffering and even if there's no reward at the end.*" Jesus isn't a device to get us to something more important. There isn't anything more important than Jesus. Jesus is the heart of it all. That's what faith is. It's saying I want Jesus above all else and I'll take the consequences.

Jesus is God saying to each one of us, "Your faith in *me* can be as tentative, diffident, and fragile as may be, but my faith in *you* will never waver, not for one single second." When God says this to you once, saying it again doesn't make it more true. God says this to us in Jesus. Once God's said it, it remains true for always.

I want to return to my two friends. To my friend who's always put off by other people's apparent certainty, I want to say, forget about how other people talk about God for a moment and just concentrate on this one question: do I want to know the power of his resurrection? Not, do I *feel* it?—remember, not even Paul could say yes to that. No, the question is, Do I *want* to know it? Do I want to know that power more than anything else in the world? That's the only question that matters. If the answer is yes, all Paul's promises can still come true for you. If the answer really is no, you may be facing a loneliness that knows no end.

To my friend who's aching for the faith he's lost, I want to say, wanting to believe *is* believing. Yearning, longing, aching to believe is entering into the passion and pathos of God's love for the world—feeling for a moment what it feels like to be God. Faith begins where certainty ends. Paul said, "I *want* to know Christ," not "I know Christ." Don't let your grief paralyze you. Let it make you bolder, more dependent than ever on the power of the resurrection. And don't let your sense of God's absence isolate you. Jesus said, "When did you see me hungry?" It sounds like you're the one who's hungry. Desperately hungry. Maybe it's time you let people see Jesus in you.

If you're like my two friends, feeling fragile in faith, take courage. Be bold in your longing to know Christ, and find ways to make that longing to know Christ a quest in which others can share and a search in which others can find a blessing. Paul's faith was tentative, as we've seen. But Paul found a way to make his longing to know Christ so infectious that it inspired all who followed. You can do the same. You don't need to hide your tentativeness and diffidence. Instead, do what Paul did; make that tentativeness and diffidence an inspiration to others. Paul's words and life became part of the Bible. By any standard, that's a big deal. But your life and words can be a kind of Bible to others if you let your life say, "More than anything else, I want to know Christ and the power of his resurrection, and I'd face any sufferings and forgo any reward if all I could know was that." Let your life speak. Let your life speak of your longing to know Christ. And let others see the resurrection in you.

# 26

# The Discipline of Joy

Afriend of mine went to medical school and at the tender age of twenty-one found himself, for the first time in his life, in a delivery room where a mother was giving birth to a baby boy. He'd always assumed that giving birth was a somewhat painful experience, so he was very surprised that the mother entered the final stages of the birth screaming, "Joy! Joy! Joy!" A couple of hours later, with the baby safely born and the mother now holding the treasured new life, my friend had the chance to speak with her. "I was so moved," he said, "to hear you shouting for joy with all your heart." "You do have a lot to learn," said the mother. "I was shouting for Joy because I was in agony. Joy's the name of the midwife."

Easter is the church's moment of joy. The good news of Easter is the best news any of us will ever hear. In Matthew's Gospel, when the angel says to the two Marys, "He has been raised," he communicates the whole gospel. Look at what these four words tell us. They tell us there's a God who is at work in Jesus. The angel doesn't say, "Jesus raised himself"—he says, "He has been raised." If we want a simple definition of God we can say "God is the one who raised Jesus from the dead." The angel's words also tell us that death's total reign is over. One has been raised. So now it's possible that all may be raised. Death was unimaginable before Adam and Eve's fall. Death can now be out-imagined because of Christ. And the angel's same words validate everything Jesus was and did in his life, ministry, and death. If he just had died on the cross, we could look at his life as a beautiful tragedy. Because he has been raised, we can look at every aspect of his life as vindicated in a way no other life has ever been. God is at work, death is defeated, everything Jesus said and did is true.

Matthew 28 gives us two parallel accounts of what Easter means. And that's very helpful, because in our faith we experience two parallel dimensions of what Easter means. On the one hand, Easter means joy, meeting Jesus face-to-face, knowing the risen Lord, enjoying all the glorious possibilities opened up by his resurrection. On the other hand, Easter means discipline, holding tight to our Easter faith even when there are no lilies, no trumpets, no heavenly choir, and life doesn't look or feel very resurrected. Joy with a profound awareness of Jesus, and the discipline of joy when we have the message of the gospel but we can't feel Jesus anywhere close: those are the two dimensions of Easter.

Matthew tells us about the discipline first. The discipline comes in the angel's appearance to the two Marys. The first thing the angel says is, "Do not be afraid" (28:5). That's the first step of the discipline of joy. Don't be afraid. Are you afraid right now? Are you afraid of that strange lump under your arm you spotted in the shower last week? Are you afraid of a mysterious comment your supervisor made a month ago about the future of your department? Are you afraid your dreams of hopeful work, happy family, and trusting friends are disintegrating around you or are never going to come true? Be not afraid. That's the first step of the discipline of joy. It's not about euphoria that blows all your worries away. It's the discipline that says, in the end, God. My life is hid with Christ in God. I never walk alone. Be not afraid.

And then the angel says, "Come, see the place where he lay" (28:6). In other words, check out the evidence for yourself. The discipline of joy isn't all about blind trust. It's about verification, scientific research, evidence-based strategic planning, and wise judgments. The Easter faith has nothing to fear from historians and scientists. "Come, see the place where he lay." The discipline of joy takes us to the places of death, despair, distress, desultory dilapidation. Do you avoid such places because they might make you feel uncomfortable, maybe even shake your faith? We don't have to keep ourselves on a high of happiness. Disciplined joy takes us instead to forsaken places, knowing those places aren't the whole story, but knowing also that those are the places where resurrection comes from.

And then the angel says, "Go quickly and tell his disciples" (28:7). In other words, this event, this experience, this faith isn't just about you. The discipline of joy means not just reflecting on your own happiness, your own sense of certainty, exhilaration, and clarity, but also having a community experience, a sharing, walking together, and discovering from one another. We go to church to look around us and see who else is in this with us and get a sense of where we can turn for comradeship when things don't seem quite so happy or straightforward.

Last, the angel says, "He is going ahead of you to Galilee; there you will see him" (28:7). In other words, the best is yet to come. Hope is the music of disciplined joy. It's the conviction that for Christians, the future is always bigger than the past. It's the determination that, whatever one's feelings, circumstances, or fears, God is our destiny, and we are being drawn to him as fragments of iron to a colossal magnet. That's what the discipline of joy means: hope, community, scrutiny, and living beyond fear.

Twenty years ago I knew a woman named Margaret who had two teenage children. One Friday her daughter didn't come home from high school. There was no word all weekend, only a message to another girl in her class, saying, "Tell my mom not to worry." Days turned to weeks, and still no word about her daughter. After six months, there was still nothing. I want you to imagine a time before cell phones and Facebook. There was no reason to suppose her daughter was dead. But no squeak from her. Then Margaret suffered an even more terrible blow. Her seventeen-year-old son came off the field after a soccer game complaining of chest pains, and there, by the side of the field, collapsed and died in front of his teammates. Margaret was alone in the world.

If ever there was a time for the discipline of joy, this was it. Margaret was devastated, but she was not afraid. She continued to check for evidence of her daughter's whereabouts. She became a Girl Scout leader and poured her love for her daughter into a community of growth and support. She kept her daughter's bedroom immaculate, because she hoped with all her heart that her daughter would come back. And one day her daughter did come back, carrying an eighteen-month-old infant boy. She marked her return with the same lack of ceremony and apology as she had marked her departure. She simply moved right back into her old bedroom as if nothing out of the ordinary had happened. But Margaret had no interest in discipline at that moment. All she had in her heart was joy. Margaret showed me what it means to live by the discipline of joy. Hope, community, scrutiny, and living beyond fear.

But that's not the whole of the Easter life. Some of Easter truly is unbridled joy. And Matthew shows us this when Jesus appears to the two Marys. Jesus begins where the angel does: "Be not afraid" (28:10). Fear gives way to joy much more quickly this time. Let's look at the joy of Easter through the two Marys' encounter with Jesus.

The joy of Easter is tangible. Matthew tells us they took hold of Jesus's feet (28:9). In other words, Jesus is not a ghost. When did you ever hear of a ghost having feet? Ghosts have long gowns, hazy complexions, shivering voices—but never feet. Jesus has feet. The two Marys take hold of one each. They see the nail marks. It's really him. He's real. Easter's real. It's not a metaphor. It's not an idea. It's not a theory. It's real. It's tangible. It's a living, breathing person. It's the crucified Jesus standing right in front of us, on the other side of death, beckoning us to the other side of death. When you feel joy, I bet your first reaction is to check your eyesight, and then hug someone. Joy is tangible. Joy hugs Jesus.

The joy of Easter is restorative. Jesus says, "Go and tell my brothers" (28:10). The angel referred to the disciples, but Jesus calls them brothers. It's not forty-eight hours since they all deserted him and fled, since Peter denied him three times—but Jesus doesn't call them former colleagues, acquaintances, or even friends—he calls them *brothers*. Already we know he forgives them. Like Joseph of Egypt, the brothers have betrayed him, he has saved them without their assistance—and now he forgives them. There's no greater joy than the joy of forgiveness. If you've never truly experienced it, then you're still to discover what Easter truly is.

The joy of Easter lies in a promise you can put your life in. Jesus says, "Tell them to go to Galilee; there they will see me." Joy isn't an all-at-one-go thing. You know how it is. You hear a sublime piece of music—then you go out and get everything by that composer. And it's too much to take in. You read a beautiful book and you buy everything that author ever wrote. And you can't swallow it when it's a mountain of books. Joy is something you taste, you touch, you glimpse—and then you have this certainty it's going to keep coming your way and it'll never run out. It's something you never get the whole of. There's always more to come. The best is yet to come. That's the joy of Easter: tangible, forgiving, growing.

Easter is about discipline and joy. The Christian life is about balancing the two. It's about the discipline of joy.

My father and mother met in Switzerland in the summer of 1955. My father's family was used to taking vacations in the Alps, and on this occasion there weren't many left in the family who weren't married off and heavy with child, so my father, who by this time was thirty-three and had been ordained in the Church of England for five years, had resorted to taking a vacation with his widowed mother, who wasn't the most lively company and wasn't a particularly energetic walker. So he was eager to make conversation, and at the next-door table he found a brother and sister. My mother's brother had won a competition for which the prize was a week's vacation in the Swiss Alps. My mother and father quickly found plenty to say to one another, and were quite happy just looking at each other when there wasn't much to say, and were delighted to find that they both had London addresses back home.

Six weeks later my father went to visit my mother's parents for Sunday high tea. After an hour my grandparents rather implausibly found that they were called away to business elsewhere. My father took his chance. Undaunted by having known my mother only six weeks, he got down on one knee in the time-honored fashion and said, "Ruth, my dear, will you marry me?" "Yes!" replied my mother, excitedly, "But . . ." and then, at this most cliffhanger of moments, the doorbell rang. It turned out that the neighbors were so intrigued by the appearance of the nice young man and the disappearance of the parents that they couldn't help but visit to find out what was going on. It took a good half hour to mollify their curiosity with platitudes.

Finally the front door closed behind them. My father, having spent the previous half hour beside himself with anxious curiosity, turned to my mother and said, "Well?" My mother opened wide her big brown eyes and said, "Well what?" "You said 'Yes, but . . .'" said my father. "What was the 'but'?" My mother paused and said, "I can't remember."

They'd had a moment of joy. They then had what seemed like an unendurable time of discipline getting used to the joy. By the time the discipline was over, no one could remember the "but." That's Easter. Living out the joy until you can't remember the "but." That's the discipline of joy.

# be not afraid of life

Before I went to seminary I was a community worker in one of the poorest neighborhoods in England. I recall meeting a young man who was very bright but hadn't had anything like the educational opportunities I'd had. He'd been baptized a Roman Catholic but never went to church, and yet he lived a life devoted to the community and to addressing its needs. I once had the courage to ask him why he never went near a church, even though the church was a great source of strength in that troubled neighborhood. His answer put me in my place. "The church is great with death," he said. "It's life it's never come to terms with."

Coming to terms with life. There are many faithful Christians who practice the faith, know the truth, keep the commandments, pursue mission in all ways, and pray for the coming of the kingdom, but somehow never evince the joy. The final part of this book is devoted to trying to articulate the joy. One may avoid such a project out of a fear of superficiality, a fear of the ephemeral character of some charismatic experiences, or a fear of overlooking the pain. But the motto of this book is "be not afraid." If one never articulated the joy, what a tragedy that would be. And the best time to speak of joy is at the end. Because Jesus at Cana, and God in the economy of salvation, saves the best till last.

# PART 6

# 27

# One Day You Will Laugh

Easter is either everything or it's nothing. It's either a doomed attempt to overcome suffering and death with lilies, drums, cymbals, brass, and a descant on the last verse, or it's a peek through a keyhole into a world completely changed by Jesus. If it's a peek through the keyhole, then the way God changes the world isn't the conventional way, through guns, bombs, war, and conquest. It's through something more dynamic than coercion, but something even more irresistible, yet more subversive, and more infectious. Something, I want to suggest, like laughter.

Have you ever noticed that animals don't laugh? Aristotle called humans the "laughing animal."[1] Laughter opens up a joy that goes beyond words. There's something divine in laughter that humanity is invited to share in. Laughing is participating in what God is (infectiously, subversively, noncoercively, but irresistibly) doing. And laughter—joyous, physically consuming, whole-body laughter—is at the heart of God.

I wonder whether you've ever been so overcome with laughter that it almost hurt. If you think about the words we use for hilarity, they're very physical, almost uncomfortable, words. We talk

1. Aristotle, *On the Parts of Animals*, bk. 3, chap. 10.

about laughing our heads off, being convulsed, having hysterics, splitting our sides, cracking up, doubling over, even *dying* laughing. There's no doubt laughing is a whole-body experience like almost no other. Both of my children were born prematurely, and both of them, coming from a clergy home, began their bid for freedom on a Sunday morning. In each case the previous evening my wife and I had laughed so much that we cried. I'm convinced the laughter brought on the birth each time.

But there's more than one kind of laughter. One thing I discovered about myself as a pastor early on was that when I was worried, or sad, or embarrassed—particularly when I was embarrassed—my first resort would often be to try to be funny and make a joke of it. Needless to say a lot of the attempts at humor fell on stony ground. Then I got more embarrassed. Eventually I realized that if I was going to be much of a pastor, it was a habit I needed to let go of. After all, being a pastor means giving people the confidence that whether they're discovering despair or joy, the truth of God or the terror of emptiness, they can do it in the presence of someone who won't be out of his or her depth. I realized my jokes were a kind of graveyard humor. What they were really indicating was that I was out of my depth.

There are a lot of different ways to use laughter as a defense. Some people laugh involuntarily every time they say anything. Some people giggle nervously so that no one might ever see them as a threat. Other people have a stock of phrases that avoid a conversation getting too serious, like "May never 'appen" or "Worse things happen at sea." All of these are self-defense mechanisms, designed to prevent the conversation becoming threatening or getting too close to the bone.

Sometimes the defensive kind of laughter is all too necessary. It's amazing how much laughter you find in places of dire poverty or oppression. In these situations a sense of humor often means the ability to see irony, incongruity, and paradox, and so realize that the world isn't a conspiracy against you. When you look back on the times you've split your sides laughing, I wonder how many of those occasions were in fact during difficult times in your life, when somehow the explosion of laughter was a gushing release of pent-up frustration, disappointment, or hurt. Think of a group of fighter pilots the night before a World War II air battle, so full of fear and anticipation, not bearing to think about danger, so convulsed with laughter about stories from home. This kind of laughter is a defense—a kind of drug that prevents you having to think about reality. It's great. But it's not real.

Of course, there's another kind of laughter. This second kind of laughter isn't about defense. It's about attack. There is a lot of this kind of laughter in the account of Jesus's crucifixion. The soldiers mock Jesus by putting a crown of thorns on his head. The chief priests mock Jesus by saying, "He saved others; he cannot save himself." The passersby mock Jesus by saying, "You talked about destroying the temple, but you can't even get yourself down from the cross." Even the bandits crucified next to Jesus mock and taunt him. It's all a big laugh.

Probably most humor is of this kind—laughing *at* other people. Whether it's the most basic slapstick banana-peel humor or more sophisticated satirical cartoons, the purpose is the same. We feel just that little bit better about ourselves and the world when we see the other guy is really pretty foolish, and the release of tension and sense of reversal makes us laugh. We feel bad about it when we shouldn't need the reassurance, when the person ridiculed is in a bad way, and we realize our laughter is a kind of gratuitous punishment willed by our small ego or our deep-seated cruelty. But when the other guy is famous, powerful, or oppressive, humor is often the best, most dynamic, and most successful way of getting one up or one back.

There's a famous story in Britain about the night former Prime Minister Margaret Thatcher took all twenty-five members of her cabinet out for dinner. The table attendant said, "What would you like to order, madam?" Mrs. Thatcher said, "Steak, please." "And the vegetables?" said the table attendant. "They'll have steak too," said Mrs. Thatcher.

This story isn't just a comment on her leadership style; it's a ridiculing of politicians as a whole. This is the laughter of revenge or subversion. Sometimes it's the laughter of pent-up hatred, deep-seated loathing, long-contained fear. Remember the pictures of Saddam Hussein's statue being toppled in Baghdad after the invasion of Iraq? For all the poignancy of the scene, what made it memorable was that it was just plain funny to watch this great dictator keel over like a child's toy.

Think about these two kinds of laughter for a moment. One is the laughter of defense, of denial, of distraction, of wishing reality were not so demanding and dangerous. The other is the laughter of attack, of the determination to have the last word, make the other guy look small, win the verbal war, humiliate anyone who threatens your territory, cut the world down to less than your size. The first kind says, life is too much for me, I want to hide or pretend. The other says, life is a war, and if I don't lash out I'll get crushed.

This is the world we live in. A world where half the time we're in denial and the other half we're at war. Half the time it's flight; half the time it's fight. This is the world of work. This is the world of home. This is the world of leisure. This is the world of nature.

This is the world that Jesus came into. And what Jesus brought was a different kind of laughter. It's an infectious laughter. A laughter of a tiny baby in a manger going *gurgle gurgle . . . hic*. A laughter of a woman finding a lost coin. A laughter of a blind man who begins to see for the first time and starts to separate the people from the trees. A laughter of Lazarus coming out of the tomb, trying to get all the death bandages off in one long peel, as if he were unraveling a tangerine. A playful laughter that doesn't humiliate or dominate, a laughter that doesn't deflect or deny. A laughter that's more infectious than a disease, more irresistible than an army, more subversive than a guerilla movement. A laughter that looks into the heart of God and smiles uncontrollably. Two days after the greatest catastrophe there has ever been or ever will be—the betrayal and execution of the Lord of glory—Easter erupts, laughing, infectiously, uncontrollably, in a way that diminishes no one, denies nothing, leaves no one out, and understands all things.

The Easter mystery contains some of the most baffling words in the whole of Christian tradition. The ancient Catholic Mass of the day includes the words, "Oh, happy fault! Oh, necessary sin of Adam! That won for us so great a salvation!" "Oh, happy fault!" It seems an insult to laugh in the face of the world's history of sin and suffering. It seems in some ways inappropriate to celebrate Jesus's resurrection when so much of God's world lies on the cross or in the tomb. But see how gripped we are by those two rival versions of laughter, laughter on the one hand as denial of reality, and laughter on the other hand as mockery and revenge.

178

Imagine a very different kind of laughter. Imagine a laughter that can't be contained, that's so infectious and so irresistible that it bursts out of the tomb and floods the whole world. It's a laughter that shakes your whole body, that splits your aching sides, that takes the head off your grief, that makes you rock deep down inside. And it's not just you, it's everybody, it's everything; the whole earth is overcome by joy, rocking and convulsing and aching with joy. The worst that humanity can do in denial and destruction has been met with irresistible laughter, not mocking, not deflecting, but laughter that creates a bigger community, tells a greater story, imagines a bigger world, laughs in tune with the laughter of God.

St. Paul talks in Romans 8 about the groaning of creation, waiting with eager longing to be set free. Even more profound than groaning is the laughter of creation, laughter deep down inside the core of all things, let loose when the stone rolls from the tomb Easter morning. Back in the 1970s in Britain there was a glam rock group called Status Quo, so famous they were known as The Quo. Those of us who wore black leather jackets had The Quo written on the back of them. (Not me, you understand.) Those of us who wore backpacks to school had black ink over the back of those rucksacks with The Quo written on them. (Not me, you understand.) But I have to confess I was one of those who sang with them, both in the '70s and then at the Live Aid concert in 1985. "And I like it, I like it, I like it, I like it, I li-li-like it, li-li-like it, here we go-oh. . . . Rockin' all over the world."[2] That was The Quo—Status Quo. Now from Easter Day forward there is a new status quo. The status quo really has changed. The whole world is rocking, rocking all over, rocking all over with laughter, the irresistible, subversive, infectious laughter of God.

Way back at the start of the Bible Sarah laughed when she was told she would have a baby. Her laughter was part defensive and part mocking. But Abraham and Sarah *did* have a son, and that son stands at the head of all God's people. At God's command Abraham took that son to Mount Moriah, making *defensive* answers when his son

2. "Rockin' All Over the World," original song by John Fogerty, rearranged and recorded by Status Quo for their album *Rockin' All Over the World*, Vertigo Records 9102 014, 1977, 33⅓, LP.

asked why, and finally in *aggressive* fashion picking up a knife to slay his son. And God intervened and said, "Enough," and Abraham's son lived and became the source of life to God's people. If that son had not lived, there would have been no Bible, no people of God. And Christians since earliest days have seen the story of Abraham and his son as the story of Good Friday and Easter. Because God's son, in his new life after sacrifice, becomes God's source of life to all people. And the name of Abraham's son was Isaac. And Isaac means "laughter."

Jesus said, "Blessed are you who weep and mourn, for one day you will laugh." When I hear laughter I think of my father. As a child I used to creep along the upstairs landing and peer through the banisters. I used to hear voices from the sitting room. My father would be chairing another smoke-filled meeting. And then, sure enough, after all had gone silent, every time there would be a peal of side-splitting laughter, my father bursting forth like a fountain of joy, infectious, irresistible, thrilling. But in the last twenty years of his life, that coruscating laughter would always be abruptly curtailed by body-wrenching coughs, coughs of the chest pains and asthma that would eventually kill him. So for me I almost always half expect laughter to be interrupted by the cough of death; I find myself looking around for the shadow of Good Friday.

But not at Easter. At Easter I can hear my father laughing again, and the laughing never stops. At Easter it's so infectious that the whole world joins in—laughing with God and with one another, laughing with the creation come alive again—one great tidal wave of joy.

On Good Friday we weep and mourn. One day, we are told, we will laugh. And we get a glimpse of what that day for laughing is like. That glimpse is called Easter.

# 28

# What Am I Going to Do
# with My Life?

When I was in middle school I had a close friend who used to run out onto the grass, hurl herself down, look up to heaven, shake her fists and kick her heels into the ground almost as if she were having a seizure, and say, "What am I going to do with my *life*?" At the time I thought it was quite funny. Now I look back with a good deal more compassion. I think she had quite understandably picked up the idea that school was supposed to give her the tools she needed to get life under control. But she already knew that her life was out of control. She already knew that she didn't have the brains to talk or think her way to success, she didn't have the looks or athletic ability to charm or float her way through life, and she didn't have the family money or stability to buy her way out of trouble or wait for someone to rescue her. Her life was out of her control, and at the age of thirteen she already knew it.

I now believe that the difference between her and most of the other people I have met in my life is that she had the courage to say it—or in her case, shout it. As Henry David Thoreau said, most people "lead lives of quiet desperation."[1] And that's true for those who are well endowed with brains, looks, money, or athletic ability—or even all four. Many of us may not shake fists, bang heels, and shout, but we nonetheless feel that life is out of control. Maybe you are one of them. If so, Matthew's Gospel has a story for you.

Matthew 3 describes how Jesus came to be baptized. We have already been told that locust-eating John was baptizing at the Jordan. Now, the Jordan isn't any old river. The Jordan is where Joshua brought the children of Israel into the Promised Land. The Jordan is where Israel left the misery of slavery and the wilderness of doubt and sin behind and entered the glorious liberty of the children of God. The River Jordan was, in other words, the place where Israel itself had been baptized, around fifteen hundred years before John the Baptist was born. And here is John, saying it's time Israel was baptized again, because Israel is in a bad way. The Romans represent Israel's slavery, and the Pharisees and Sadducees in different ways represent Israel's sin. And John is a voice crying in the wilderness—that's the same wilderness, remember, where Israel was before it came into a land of its own.

Jesus chooses this moment to begin his ministry. Like Israel, he's been down in Egypt. Like Israel, he enters his inheritance at the River Jordan. John says to Jesus, "Hold your horses, you aren't the oppressive Romans and you aren't the failed Jewish leadership: why are you coming to be baptized?" And Jesus replies, "No, I'm not here because I need to be saved from sin or released from slavery. I'm here because I'm Israel. I'm the one on whom the hope of Israel and the hope of the world rests. And if I'm going to be Israel, I have to do what Israel has to do. I have to be baptized. It's not about ending something bad; it's about beginning something wonderful."

John quickly realizes he's going to lose the argument, so he gets down to business. And stay tuned for what happens next because it's a condensed version of everything God has in store for Jesus, Israel, and you and me. "Suddenly the heavens were opened to [Jesus] and he saw the Spirit of God descending like a dove and alighting on him. And a voice from heaven said, 'This is my Son, the Beloved, with whom I am well pleased'" (Matt. 3:16b–17). These two sentences

---

1. Henry David Thoreau, *Walden* (Boston: Ticknor and Fields, 1854; New York: Library Classics of the United States, 2010), 9.

give us the whole shape of the biblical story, and they tie together Jesus's story with Israel's story. Let me explain.

What does the picture of a dove coming over water make you think of? It's Noah's dove, of course. Remember Noah sent out the dove, and it came back empty-beaked. He sent out the dove again, and it came back with a twig, little knowing it would thus provide an image to be printed on T-shirts and Happy Holidays cards for eternity. Noah sent out the dove a third time, and the dove didn't come back. That meant the waters had subsided. Then God sent the rainbow to say the earth would never be destroyed again. But that made a problem for God. The earth was still full of sin, but God had ruled out destroying the earth again. As the Old Testament relates, God tried a few ways of addressing the problem. But the appearance of the dove shows us that Jesus is God's ultimate answer to the problem. At Jesus's baptism, Noah's dove finally comes back. Salvation literally comes home to roost. And then we realize, if we hadn't already, that the story of Noah is a baptism story. God drowns sin in water, and the dove marks the beginning of the emergence of a new humanity out of the water. So we see that Jesus's baptism stands in relation to Matthew's Gospel the way Noah stands in relation to the Old Testament. It's the creation of a new humanity.

And then we notice that Matthew tells us the dove is the Holy Spirit. Holy Spirit . . . over the surface of the water. . . . Make you think of anything? Genesis 1:2 says the Spirit of God hovered over the face of the waters. So to mention a dove points us to Noah, and to mention the Spirit over the water tells us this is a new-creation story. When we look at the virginal conception of Jesus (Matt. 1:18–25) we discover that that was also a new-creation story. Then as now the Holy Spirit hovered over and alighted on someone, and then as now there was a new creation out of nothing. This isn't a coincidence. Matthew doesn't do coincidences. It's Matthew telling us that there were two beginnings to the Old Testament, the beginning in creation and the new beginning in the covenant with Noah. And in just the same way there were two new beginnings for Jesus, the amazing birth and here, now, the inspired baptism. And the same is true for our own lives: there are two beginnings, the birth from the womb of our mother and the rebirth in baptism from the womb of God.

At this moment there is a voice from heaven that says, "This is my beloved son." Now, there's only one place in the whole of the Old Testament where these two words, *beloved* and *son*, are used together. It's not in Isaiah. It's not in the Psalms. It's not in the Song of Songs. It's at the scariest place of all—the moment that sends shivers down the spine of the Old Testament. Genesis 22. The moment when God calls on Abraham to take Isaac to Mount Moriah to sacrifice him there. God says to Abraham, "Take your son, your *beloved son*, and offer him as a burnt offering." As we know, Abraham obeyed and was at the point of killing his son when God intervened and offered a ram instead. Christians have long seen Jesus both as that son and also as the lamb of God whose sacrifice saves us. And we get this foreshadowing of the cross at the moment of Jesus's baptism, in these words *beloved son*. God's words to Abraham, and now God's words to Jesus. We've already seen Jesus's and John's obedience in going ahead with the baptism. Obedience was Abraham's great virtue. Now we see Abraham again in these words *beloved son*.

Abraham. When I mentioned the two beginnings in the Old Testament I spoke too soon. There are, in fact, *three* beginnings. *Creation*, yes, *covenant* with Noah, yes, but then Abraham—the *call* of Abraham is another beginning. Jesus's birth recalls creation. His baptism echoes Noah. And his call to the cross is hinted at in these words that follow his baptism, and that call reminds us of Abraham—God's third new beginning.

We already have a hint that Jesus's journey to the cross will not be in vain, because we are told that heaven is open. Jesus's obedience to his call to be the new Israel leads to John's obedience, and then the heavens open, in anticipation of what Jesus achieves for us in his resurrection from the dead. Now, we've all seen James Bond films, and we can all imagine some kind of automatic door opening above our heads, operated by some evil genius who not only plans to kill 007 and rule the world but also wears black leather gloves and has a pathological fondness for technical gadgets. But I don't think heaven opening is like that. Heaven opening means that for a fleeting moment the distance between us and God is taken away and God is all in all. For a precious instant the earth is full of the grandeur of God and everything is bursting with God's promise and glory. Just for a moment heaven is open to earth and earth is open to heaven, just as it will be at the end of time.

The climax of all this dazzling reconfiguration of the Old Testament in the person of Jesus at the moment of his baptism comes in the very last words that God speaks. "I am *overjoyed* with him." This again is the fruit and result of Jesus's ministry, and it is anticipated here at its outset: God is overjoyed with us. Not because we are so fabulous in ourselves, with all our brains, looks, money, or athletic prowess, but because whenever God looks on us he sees Jesus. And so God is overjoyed with us, because Jesus is humanity in perfect relationship with God. Imagine heaven opening and God saying, "I am overjoyed with you."

One of the saddest stories I ever heard was of a woman called Fiona. Her father was in the most elite battalion of the British army. Like my friend in middle school, she was utterly bewildered, but, unlike my friend, she knew why. She was angry. She was angry because she felt she could never be good enough for her father. Instead of going to college, she embarked on a walk. A long walk. The walk lasted eleven years. It took her much of the way around the world. Toward the end she was invited to talk to a group of third graders in a local class. She said, "You know, sometimes when you're walking home from school you are cross and you just decide to take the longer route home." One of the children said, "Eleven years is a very long route home." Fiona replied, "Yes. I was very cross. Very, very cross." Finally she took the boat back to England. She returned to a hero's welcome after a remarkable feat of physical and spiritual endurance. There was only one person she was longing to meet. Her father. Her father came to meet her on a hill in Cornwall. It'd been a long time. He handed her his military beret, symbol of his achievements in the army. And as she told the story, she wept, and said, "but I didn't deserve it."

Nothing, it seemed, could convince her that she was good enough for her father. And that shows us the wonder of these last words in the story of Jesus's baptism: "I am well pleased." God is overjoyed with us. Not because we're so wonderful but because Jesus is.

This brings us to see how the baptism of Jesus tells us not just Israel's story, not just Jesus's story, but our own story. We may well shake our fists and kick our heels and shout, "What am I going to do with my *life*?" We may well feel that the bits of life that matter are well out of control. But God made three new beginnings with Israel and embodied those three new beginnings in Jesus at the moment of his baptism. And he makes those three new beginnings in us.

First of all, God is our *creator*. God made you this way because he wanted one like you. In some ways you are like everyone else, like everything else—you are an earthly, contingent part of the created order. But there are things that you can be and do that others can't, because of your unique experience, your unique history, your unique shape of body, mind, and spirit. And there is something in the world that only you can do, something that will remain undone until you appear to do it, something that God created you to do. You may not yet know what that unique thing is. The important thing is that when the moment comes, you're ready.

Second, God makes a *covenant* with you. Just as with Noah. This is what baptism embodies. God could do it alone, but the covenant means that God longs to do it with you. If creation means God is delighted with you, then covenant means God expects something of you. The covenant is simply this. God has given everything to you—your life and his. He expects everything from you in return. Faith isn't a spectator sport—it's about participating in the way God makes a new beginning. Keeping the covenant isn't about getting everything right in such a way as it seems you could do it without God. Keeping the covenant means faithfully and honestly getting it wrong in such a way as to make room for God to clean up afterward.

Finally, God *calls* you. And if it's anything like God's call to Abraham, which it will be, it will at some stage feel very much like a call to walk with Jesus on the way to the cross. If creation makes you know you matter, and covenant helps you know God is with you, call means being taken from the place, people, habits, or paths that you know and being taken to a new place, people, role, or challenge. In the New Testament, as soon as someone is baptized, they are given a new job to do, and that job always takes them, sooner or later, literally or metaphorically, to the cross. In Jesus's baptism we discover the way God calls us. God calls us with the words, "My beloved child." God calls us as the one who made us for a reason. And God calls us as the one who will never leave us alone.

We may well ask the question, what am I going to do with my life? But the more interesting question is, what is *God* going to do with your life? God created you, and in baptism makes a covenant with you. Stay close to the way God communicates with you. Stay close to Scripture, stay close to wise and truthful friends, stay close to the poor, stay close to beauty, stay close to worship, stay close to the cross. And be expecting a call.

# 29

# Loving Yourself

Y ou're on the phone. The conversation is getting pretty intense. The voice says, "I need you to come." You pause. You say, "I'm sorry, I can't come right now." The voice says, "But you said you didn't have plans for this weekend." You pause a bit longer, on a knife-edge between emotional exhaustion and nagging guilt. You say, "I'm sorry, I need a bit of time to myself." "Okay," says the voice, bitterly. "I get the message." Ouch. Nagging guilt wins again.

I have a hunch that you've had that phone call. You know that tussle between nagging guilt and emotional exhaustion. After the words "Okay, I get the message," the trump card, spoken or unspoken, is "I thought you were supposed to be a Christian."

Because being a Christian is taken to mean, "permanently open to emotional exhaustion, physical burnout, psychological manipulation, and relentless guilt." Prepared to go to any lengths, in fact, to avoid being called "selfish." Two hundred years ago the French philosopher Auguste Comte coined the term *altruism*. Altruism means living a life for others. Since then a great many people have assumed altruism was what Christianity was really all about. We all know people who seem to say, "Because I'm worn out being so noble to others, that makes it okay for me to be short-tempered, mean, and ungenerous to you." Altruism assumes that in order to love others more, you need to love yourself less. It takes love to be a zero-sum game, where if you give in one place you have to take away somewhere else. This is a grim view of the world in which someone always has to suffer, and love means that that someone should be you.

When you're on the phone to the person who wants more from you than you can give, the assumption is there are only two options—altruism or selfishness. I want to see how Jesus helps us with that phone call by introducing us to something called self-love. In Matthew 22:36, Jesus is asked, "Which commandment in the law is the greatest?" And he replies, "'You shall love the Lord your God with all your heart, and with all your soul, and with all your mind.' This is the greatest and first commandment. And a second is like it: 'You shall love your neighbor as yourself'" (22:37–39). I want to isolate the key words in this answer: *God, neighbor, self,* and *love.* What Jesus's words show us is that we can't grasp what it means to love *ourselves* appropriately until we've got a sense of *God* and *neighbor.*

Let's start with *God.* Jesus says, "Love the *Lord your God.*" Every word counts. This isn't a distant abstract God who set the universe in motion and then took a long lunch break. This is the *Lord.* That's the God whose name was so holy Israel couldn't say it out loud, whose face was so wondrous they couldn't look upon it, whose heart was so passionate they wrote book after book about it in the face of their faltering response. And this Lord is *your* God. The whole gospel is in that little word *your.* Your God means the God who shaped his whole life to be in relationship with you, not just in the good times but when you've completely messed up and when it's all shocking, embarrassing, humiliating, and sad. Have you ever heard a tiny child scream out "Daddy!" or "Mommy!" at the top of his or her voice in a moment of pure joy or need, matched by complete confidence that his or her parent is entirely present and entirely devoted to him or her? We're as close to God as that child to that parent. That's the power of the word *your.* Jesus doesn't talk about God; he talks about the *Lord your* God.

That brings us to the word *neighbor.* When elsewhere Jesus is asked the famous question, who is my neighbor? we immediately sense the panic that the command to love is simply an invitation to be overwhelmed. We're not sure if the neighbor means the regular

189

people we encounter, the poor, the enemy, or the whole wide world. It sounds like a recipe for either naive sentimentalism or manic burnout. The political right talks about responsibility for individual neighbors, but that sounds like shorthand for lowering taxes. The political left talks as if loving your neighbor is something you can arrange for the government to do on your behalf.

The trouble is, because we're unclear about these words *God* and *neighbor*, we have no idea what to say about ourselves. This brings us to the word *self.* To use academic jargon, you could say the project of modernity is to create a freestanding self that doesn't need God or neighbor. How's this project going, I wonder. Well, despite airport bookstores crammed with self-help manuals, limitless advice on what diet and activities will benefit your toddler, and a reduction in the chronic wars, famines, and diseases that used to keep earlier generations busy, we don't seem to have got any happier. With increasing affluence, we have fewer things to blame for the confused selves that we still have. So we blame . . . our parents. As the poet Philip Larkin points out in his poem "This Be the Verse," our parents make a mess of our lives: "They may not mean to, but they do. / They fill you with the faults they had / And add some extra, just for you."[1] Our parents can't escape: if it's nature, it's their genes that we blame; if it's nurture, we simply blame them for being too strict or too lenient, too distant or too smothering. They only have one resort: they get to blame their own parents. In some cases this turns out to be a watertight excuse. But having someone to blame isn't a solution to the problem of self-love. It's just a sign that the project of creating a self that doesn't need God or neighbor isn't going too well.

So what has Christianity to say on the subject? For Christians, God and neighbor come as a package deal in the figure of Jesus. Jesus shows us what God looks like, the *Lord* God, whose life is shaped to be with us, the Lord *our* God, who's as close to us as a mother to her baby. And Jesus shows us what our neighbor looks like. The good Samaritan parable comes alive when we realize it is *Jesus* who was beaten, bruised, and left to die. That's what the cross did—it left Jesus dying by the side of the road; it made Jesus our neighbor.

1. Philip Larkin, *High Windows* (London: Faber and Faber, 1974), 30.

And it is *us* who walk past on the other side, then and now. When Jesus says, "Whatever you did for the hungry, the naked, and the prisoner, you did for me" (Matt. 25:34–40), he is showing us himself in our neighbor. So when Jesus says, "You shall love the Lord your God with all your heart, and with all your soul, and with all your mind. . . . And you shall love your neighbor as yourself" (Matt. 22:37, 39), *he* is the Lord our God, and *he* is our neighbor.

So there's only one place to go to form an understanding of ourselves. There's only one place to stand, and that's face-to-face with Jesus. You are not your wallet; you are not your house; you are not your car; you are not your GPA—you are not even your family. You are what Jesus thinks of you, because Jesus is God, and Jesus is your neighbor. You can never fully know yourself, but you can be fully known: Jesus knows you better than you know yourself. Jesus is hurt by thoughtless things you never knew you'd done, and delighted by unconscious gestures you never realized you'd made. He understands the fear that makes you cruel and the joy that makes you generous. He rejoices in the very thrill of your existence, is tender and close to you when you are curved in on yourself, is overjoyed in the very moment of your repentance, is exultant as you spread your wings to fly in his Spirit. Jesus is the heart within your heart. And he adores you.

If none of this were true, of course we'd be selfish. Selfishness says, "No one's looking out for me, so I'd better take as much as I can, while I can, so I have plenty for when things turn bad." Selfishness says, "The truth about me is terrible, so I'm going to get all I can and pig out all I can until someone finds out the truth about me and the game's up." Selfishness isn't a sign of too much self-love: it's quite the opposite. It's a sign of profound insecurity. It's a moment of panic that says there's no eternal assurance and so I must grab and go. As a pastor, when I see a person acting in a way that seems deeply selfish, I try to ask them, "Is this really what you want? Is this really making you happy?" Usually the answer is no. And amazingly often there are tears. I see it as an opportunity more often for compassion than for condemnation.

For those of you who have always been told that you should live for others and always put others before yourself or risk being called selfish, here's a word of advice. When you hear the words, "Love your neighbor as yourself," swap the words around and say, "Love yourself as your neighbor." In other words, regard yourself as the first among all the neighbors God calls you to love. God's got a lot to be doing with the whole creation, but the wonderful thing is, God has chosen to start with you. The language of altruism never really grasps this. It makes loving others seem impossibly hard work, because it assumes that you have to choose between loving yourself and loving others. But God loves every one of us while still loving each of us as if we were the only one. We're able to love others because of the way God loves us. And to accept that love, we have to learn to love ourselves. This is the final key word in the command to love the neighbor: *love*.

I wonder if you've ever served meals in a restaurant, café, or even to a large family. You know how a meal can be ruined if the person serving it is crotchety, distracted, or generally in a bad mood. If you're that person, it pays to eat at least a small snack or meal earlier yourself so you're in the right frame of mind to serve a meal to others. If your stomach is rumbling, or your tongue's hanging out as you serve up the supper, you aren't going to be much help to your guests. You love others best by loving yourself first. And think of the way you pray. So many of us have been told to pray the way we serve food, to pray for everyone else first and leave ourselves until last. The trouble is we've usually got something huge on our mind that stops us from concentrating on anyone else. Much better to pray for yourself first, get it out and done, and then wholeheartedly get on with laying out before God the people we know in distress and the passion and pain around them.

This is the work of self-love: to let yourself be loved by Jesus, and to be so energized and transformed by that love that you love yourself as the first among all the countless neighbors God calls you to love. To learn to be their friend, you practice by being your own friend. You don't resent those neighbors, because they're not taking away anything that belongs to you. You've already been looked after, because after being loved by Jesus, there's nothing more to want. By contrast, if you're looking elsewhere to bolster your self-regard, I've got bad news for you: it will never be enough. It will be like pouring water into a jug with a leak at the bottom. Of course that's exhausting. In that economy, looking after yourself is bound to take away from looking after others. But when the love of Jesus has made you something or someone you never dared imagine you could be, has made you beautiful despite your blemishes, has made you good despite your betrayals, has made you true despite your lies, then self-love is simply a happy introduction to a story that isn't finally about you.

Let's go back to that phone call. Remember, the best way I can to teach you to love *yourself* is to love *myself*, because being a Christian requires me to love myself as I love you. We left the call where you say, "I'm sorry, I need a bit of time to myself." "Okay," says the voice, bitterly. "I get the message. . . . I thought you were supposed to be a Christian." Maybe this is what your friend needs to hear: "If you go on like this, in your insecurity, looking anxiously for appreciation, you're going to make yourself and others miserable. You'll live in the wilderness, wandering unhappily, searching desperately for the affirmation that never sufficiently comes. You'll be a nomad, demanding from everyone, yet belonging nowhere. You're greedily seeking attention for yourself and when you don't get it you're calling people names for not satisfying your limitless demands. The truth is, I can't give you what you most deeply need. You're asking something from me that only God can give.

"And God is longing to give it to you. You've tried to build yourself up on your own strength and on other people's approval. It's not working. Maybe it's time you learned to accept that God adores you. God knows you inside out and still adores you. If you can only accept that, then you won't be looking for affirmation and approval from me and others like me all the time. You'll begin to see yourself as God sees you, gloriously made, profoundly confused, but bursting with gifts and delights. You'll stop looking relentlessly for rewards and recognition. You'll discover that the kingdom of heaven is yours. You'll never be an exile and never be in the wilderness. You'll be everywhere at home. And you'll have nothing that you weren't longing to share with friend and stranger.

"Speak to you after the weekend."

# 30

# A Criminal Waste

You never regret your extravagances. God is wild and free, and God made us to be wild and free too. Hard as we try, we will never succeed in domesticating God.

Despite being just 5'2", Alison Hargreaves was widely regarded as one of the best climbers in the world. When aged twenty-six, she conquered the formidable north face of the Eiger in the Swiss Alps. Afterward some criticized her for climbing while six months pregnant with her first child. Her explanation was terse. "I was pregnant, not sick," she replied. Five years on she was the first person to climb, by herself, and in one season, the six north faces of the Alps. Two years later, in 1995, when she was thirty-three, she set out to climb the world's three highest mountains in one summer. She became the first female, and the second person, to climb to the top of Mount Everest without porters, without climbing partners, and without extra oxygen. Not long after, she conquered Pakistan's fearsome K2. But during the descent from the summit of K2, she and her five companions were lost in a blizzard. They never made it down. When her husband was given the news, he simply said, "I can hear her repeating her favorite saying, 'One day as a tiger is better than a thousand years as a sheep.'"[1]

Alison Hargreaves mixed an incredible will, an astonishing thirst for climbing, a commitment to detail and technique, and a raging passion for the mountains. Now, not all of us are quite like her. For some of us the mere prospect of an overnight camping expedition is enough to send us scurrying for the air conditioning, dishwashers, and blow-dryers that soften our encounter with the great outdoors. But I believe Jesus enjoys the Alison Hargreaves of this world. And his encounter with Mary of Bethany at the house of Martha and Lazarus tells us why.

In John 12, Jesus is sitting down to dinner with Lazarus, Martha, and a bunch of friends. Mary, the sister of Martha and Lazarus, takes a full pound of exquisite perfume and pours it over Jesus's feet. Now I don't know how many people have found themselves stuck without a Christmas present for a loved one on the day before Christmas Eve. Quite likely you're terrified of going up to a perfume counter because you think they'll offer you a host of products you don't know the names of in sizes you haven't heard of and in shapes of bottles you can't understand. So this is what you do. You treat it like old-fashioned vegetable shopping, and say, "I'll take a pound of pure nard, please." Right? Wrong. A pound is an *astronomical* amount of perfume.

Our old friend Brother Judas Iscariot happens to be lurking around the back of the party, keeping an eye on the goings-on. Clearly he's got a better sense of the market price of perfume than your average disciple. He takes one look at it and reckons it's worth 300 denarii. Let's do a quick bit of math. A denarius was the average pay for one day's work. If the average household income in the United States today is around $50,000, then we're saying the perfume Mary poured over Jesus's feet that night was worth the equivalent of $40,000. Forty thousand dollars' worth of perfume! I don't care what your bailout package or stimulus plan is for the local ointment trade: that's an unbelievable amount of money.

You've got to have a bit of sympathy for Judas. That's an outrageous sum of money. Feel the eyes of the whole room. Watch

1. "Alison Hargreaves," Gale Encyclopedia of Biography, www.answers.com/topic/alison-hargreaves.

everyone's eyeballs popping out of their head as they see a bottle of perfume with a whole *pound* of expensive scent in it. "Don't drop that! Watch what you're doing with it! Take it easy! Hold on!" There's the sheer mesmerizing fascination of seeing $40,000 of liquid wrapped up in such a fragile container, held by such delicate hands. Where on *earth* did Mary get the money to buy such a massive quantity of perfume? Is this her, her brother's, and her sister's retirement savings, all thrown into one precarious investment?

And then, what's this? She's kneeling at Jesus's feet. Now you don't know where to look. Women don't touch men in this culture. They certainly don't touch a man's foot, because everyone knows a foot might just as well be what we could politely call an upper, inner thigh. This is a disgraceful public performance. And now she's picking up the bottle of perfume, and she's *pouring it all over Jesus's feet*. That's unbelievable! What a terrible waste. Making erotic gestures in front of everybody is one thing—but squandering a huge sum of money is quite another. I can't believe she's just poured $40,000 all over the floor! And now she's wiping Jesus's feet with her hair! What a performance! She seems to have no shame about the flagrant indecency, no awareness of the public disgrace, and no worries whatsoever about the criminal waste of money.

Judas is indignant. "Why was this perfume not sold for three hundred denarii and the money given to the poor?" (John 12:5). Whatever his personal motives, you miss the force of the story unless you recognize that Judas has a very important point. It's not just that this is a lot of money and it could benefit a lot of people. It's that the Jerusalem temple, as well as being the key place where Jews could find their sins forgiven and be close to God's heart, was also the center of a bureaucracy that managed welfare on behalf of the poor. So Judas isn't just being mean or greedy. He's saying, "We already *have* a system for managing welfare. And this woman has just driven a coach and horses through it in a disgraceful, profligate, and insulting manner. What on earth does she think she's doing? And what on earth do *you* think you're doing *letting* her?"

Judas offers us the voice of common sense, of decency, of public order. Don't waste precious money and resources. Don't step too close to the boundaries of proper relations between the sexes. Don't bypass the very carefully thought-out systems for providing welfare benefits for the truly poor. Who are we to disagree with Judas? He has all the vocabulary that makes our lives function: stewardship, policies and procedures, bylaws, strategic plans. And yet he can't see the one thing that's staring him in the face. He can't see the one thing that Mary alone *can* see: that Jesus is going to die in a week's time. There may of course be good reasons why Judas isn't prepared to see that. Judas is going to have a big hand in Jesus's entrapment. But the point is, besides Mary, no one else is seeing it either.

Now, finally, we are in a position to make sense of the whole scene. I wonder if you've ever been in a community or in a relationship where everyone else that mattered is so preoccupied, so taken up with themselves, the usual way of doing things, or a bunch of trivial or superficial politenesses, that you felt like taking all your clothes off and screaming at the top of your voice and doing something really crazy to get their attention. That's pretty much what Mary does. And even when she does, *still* no one pays the slightest bit of attention. All that happens is that Judas points out that she's totally out of order. And Jesus says, "Leave her alone. She bought it so that she might keep it for the day of my burial. You always have the poor with you, but you do not always have me" (John 12:7–8). In other words, Jesus says, "But don't you *see*? She's behaving just like me! She's demonstrating the extravagance of human love. She's poured out her whole self—financial, social, emotional—to gain your attention by a gesture of sheer beauty. I'm demonstrating the extravagance of *divine* love. I'm pouring out my whole self—physical, spiritual, metaphysical—to gain your attention by a gesture of sheer beauty. I am the extravagance of God. And if you're taking no notice of *her*, then how much worse that you're taking no notice of *me*."

Jesus is God flinging off clothes and doing the most crazy, wild thing to get us to see what really matters. Jesus is God kicking and screaming to try to stir our attention away from the trivial and greedy distractions that bloat and suffocate our lives. Jesus is God wasting the most precious and beautiful things to show utter devotion to us. The life of Jesus is worth a lot more than 300 denarii or $40,000. And it's a total waste unless . . . unless it wins us back to God.

And that leaves us with two uncomfortable but very necessary questions. We could call them the Judas question and the Mary question. First, the Judas question. What is the thing you are not able or willing to see? What is God trying to show you? What is someone close to you trying to say to you? I wonder if there's something that somebody is trying to tell you or show you, maybe so desperately that they're starting to do crazy and ridiculous things to get your attention. I wonder if you're so taken up with routines, distractions, and defenses that you can't see them or won't hear them. I wonder if somehow all your policies, procedures, plans, and programs are, in the end, ways to avoid seeing the one thing that matters.

And then the Mary question. What is the beautiful thing you are being called to do? I wonder if there is something you are drawn to but shy away from because it seems too costly, extravagant, crazy, or ridiculous. I wonder if there is a gesture you need to make because, like Mary's gesture, it's time for you, for once in your life, to imitate the extravagance of God. I wonder if, like Mary, you've suddenly realized that this important thing has to happen right now—and it won't wait.

When other people see your life, what do they see? Do they see a criminal waste? And if they do, is that waste one that mimics Judas's parsimony or Mary's extravagance? Judas, Mary, and Jesus all wasted their lives in different ways. The point is, have you wasted your life in caution or in love? When people see the waste of your life, does it make them think of Judas or of Jesus?

Some years ago, when I was a pastor of a little church in England, there was a woman who was in her late fifties and was just for the first time learning to read. She'd grown up in a children's home and the good things in life came late to her. She worked at the local hospital taking meals around the wards on a cart. At forty she married an honest man, and her mother-in-law became the mother she'd never had. So her mother-in-law's death was a terrible blow to her. She told me, "Sam, I spoke to my supervisor, and I told her the situation, and I asked her for a couple of weeks' passionate leave." I looked at her, and I didn't know whether to laugh or cry. I said, "*Passionate* leave? Really?" The idea of this sedate, older lady enjoying a couple of weeks of unbridled passion was a bit much for my imagination. Of course, she meant to say "*com*passionate leave." (That's what bereavement leave is called in England.) But she was as beautiful and right as Mary—and I was as foolish and wrong as Judas. A couple of weeks' passionate leave was just what she needed, to recognize all that love she'd poured out for the mother she'd never had.

198

I wonder if it's time you asked for a couple of weeks' passionate leave. A week to reflect on the Judas question: what's the thing I'm desperately trying with all my busyness and politeness and professionalism not to see? And a week to reflect on the Mary question: what's the beautiful thing I'm being called to do—embarrassing, extravagant, or crazy as it may be?

Alison Hargreaves showed us the face of God because she knew her passion, and she knew the danger her passion might put her in—but, like a tiger, she let that passion lead her life. That's what God does. I wonder if you have a passion like that. God does. It's you. You are the extravagant passion of God.

You never regret your extravagances. How do I know that? Because neither does God. And what is God's extravagance? God's extravagance is you. God's expensive, gorgeous, fragrant, crazy, and ultimately useless and wasteful extravagance—is you. And God never regrets pouring out and wasting everything—for you.

# 31

# With Both Hands

I'd like you to hold both hands in front of you, palms upward, with the little finger of each hand just touching one another. Think about the Father's hands, which made the world in all its myriad complexity, glory, and wonder, and think about the detail and care that went into those hands. And now look at the center of each hand and think about the Son's hands that redeemed the world, and the nails that were rammed through each palm as he did so, and see how much the Son loved us. And now look at your two hands once more, and think about the Holy Spirit, and realize that the Holy Spirit's hands are the ones you're looking at now. That's what it means to be a Christian. That's what it means to be a disciple. That's what it means to be a missionary.

I wonder how often you use two hands. I came to America determined to understand baseball. Perhaps the symbol of baseball—perhaps the symbol of the American summer—is the large padded mitt you wear on your nonthrowing hand. You have to realize that I'm a person who's spent a lot of time trying and failing to catch a cricket ball with *two* hands, so the one-handed method makes me feel pretty small. That single baseball glove says to me, "Of course

200

I can catch and prepare to throw at the same time. We are, after all, a culture committed to multitasking."

We are indeed a culture committed to multitasking. It sometimes seems every aspect of life is being shaped so as to ensure it can be performed with one hand. We drive vehicles with automatic transmission so we always have one hand free to fight with the road map or speak on a cell phone. We eat fast food so we can have a hand free to browse the web while the other hand reaches for the french fries. We write a paper, go to a party, text message our way into a new romantic encounter, and follow the basketball score all in the same evening, or even all at the same moment. This is something we learn quite early on, at least in middle or high school, and we notice it in teenagers because they're doing several things at the same time but they haven't yet learned the art of being fully present in each one. (Of course not, we might say—you have to go to college for that.) But teenagers are really no different from the rest of us. It's as if life is a supermarket, and we have one hand on the cart while the other hand is always available to touch and sample the myriad experiences and opportunities available on one or the other side of the aisle, tossing each consumer possibility into the cart with little or no thought to the checkout.

I wonder what things make you interrupt the one-hand culture. What are the things you take with both hands? Maybe a ticket to a celebrated sporting contest or a theatrical or musical performance. Maybe a top job offer or a place at your number one graduate school. As you look back on your life, I wonder which moments have needed two hands. To put the question another way, I wonder which places you're content just to be silent—with no iPod, no conversation, and no snacking, just beauty or peace. And I wonder which people you're content to be silent with—not have great laughs, great debates, or great dancing, but just company, stillness, and companionship. Those are the places and the people with whom we can be still, through whom we can know what matters most, for whom we think it's worth using both hands.

Sixteen hundred years ago St. Augustine of Hippo distinguished between two kinds of things.[1] One kind of thing we *enjoy*. These

1. Augustine, *On Christian Doctrine*, bk. 1, chap. 3, 4, trans. J. F. Shaw (Edinburgh: T&T Clark, 1892), 9.

are the things that are worth having for their own sake. They aren't a means to an end, they're a joy in themselves. They're things that never run out. You don't have to make an argument for why they matter; they speak for themselves. The other kind of thing we *use*. Things we use aren't good in themselves; they're a means to some further end. They do run out. They serve only a limited purpose.

I want to suggest that what we grasp, take, or juggle in *one* hand is what we *use*; and what we yearn for, treasure, and shape our whole posture to receive and cherish is what we *enjoy*. What we *use* only requires one hand: we can use a number of things at the same time. But to *enjoy* something, or someone, we really need *both* hands, because it takes all our concentration.

In the story of Mary and Martha (Luke 10:38–42), we see a contrast between one-handed and two-handed culture. Martha struggles to do important tasks—tasks that don't seem quite so important when one realizes she is in the presence of Jesus. It seems Martha wants to take God with one hand while doing everything else at the same time. By contrast Mary sits at Jesus's feet, without another thought in the world—much to her sister's annoyance. For Mary, God truly is a project that needs both hands. Martha is a multitasker. Jesus inevitably becomes for her just another item in the shopping cart. Mary has only one concern in her mind—to enjoy Jesus. There's nothing else that's more important. Martha uses; Mary enjoys.

I want to say a little more about what it means to enjoy. It's easy for any Christian to see the state of the world and feel anxious that they're not doing anything worthwhile. So of course we want to show we're useful. Think about that word—*use*ful. We're busy, and full of activity, and hard to pin down. But then we're not living in God's time. Because those who live in God's time inspire people to *enjoy*, to see that life is about enjoying God the way God enjoys us. Think about how this works out in church life. Recall the moment you're at the children's vacation Bible school, and it's ten minutes before the end, and the leaders are thinking of starting to tidy up early, and a child says to you, "Does God have a face?" Don't make a joke; don't say, "I've got to tidy up"; don't give a reflex answer. Stay right where you are and *enjoy* the question. "Hmmmm. Maybe the stars are God's hair. Maybe the roses are God's nose. Maybe the waterfalls are God's beard. Maybe the oceans are God's eyes. I know what God's hands are like, because they've got scars on them, haven't they?" *Enjoy* that moment.

And let's say you're making conversation during the coffee hour and another member of the church says to you, "My husband died fifty years ago today." Don't say, "Well I never," or "Doesn't time fly," and drift away to find the cream or sweetener. Look into her eyes and say, "Do you still love him?" or "Did it break your heart?" or "Have you ever been able to love again?" Enjoy the conversation. It's what being a fellow disciple is all about. Not to get better at using—a hundred manuals and instruction booklets do that. But to share the walk of discipleship with people who are longing to enjoy and be enjoyed. To take one another with two hands, for once in our lives.

Living life with both hands takes time—because what you receive with both hands takes longer to assimilate than what you seize with one. Above all, living with two hands takes gentleness—because treasuring moments, people, or places with both hands, rather than grabbing them with one, means cherishing them, tenderly noticing their details, carefully attending to their difference from you, but rejoicing in their presence.

Notice that the distinction between *use* and *enjoy* applies to God too. God doesn't *use* us. God *enjoys* us. In other words, we're not a consumer good God tosses into the cart and thinks about dealing with later at the checkout. On the contrary, the whole life of God is shaped to be in relationship with us, to enjoy us. God never deals with us with one hand. God always approaches us with both hands—because we mean everything to God. There's nothing more important in God's life than us—there's no reason to multitask, for God's joy is *us*. The great mystery, of course, is the mystery of whether we will enjoy God in return, and shape our life in order to receive God with two hands, or simply try to use God as just one more consumer good in the shopping cart. One Reformation-era description of the Christian faith says that we were made to *enjoy God forever*.[2] That doesn't sound like a one-hander to me, however big the glove on that one hand. That's a project that needs both hands.

2. According to the Westminster Shorter Catechism of 1647, "Man's chief end is to glorify God, and to enjoy him for ever."

I don't know if you have ever seen an ibex. An ibex is a large and very rare mountain goat, about five feet tall. The male has enormous ridged horns that curve all the way around to his back. I once climbed a mountain up to twelve thousand feet and suddenly caught sight of an ibex three hundred feet away. I gently stepped closer and closer. This wasn't a moment I could grab with a quick camera shot and move on. If I was going to see the ibex close up, even though I'd already been walking six hours, I had to change my plans for the day. Softly and slowly I went closer and closer, one careful step at a time. I saw its proud chin, its huge curving horns stretching back behind its head. Finally I was twenty feet away from this prince of the mountains. And how I *enjoyed* that moment. I don't know how long I was there. But I felt so privileged, moved, and deeply, deeply alive. And it took more than two hands. It took everything in me. *That's* what it means to enjoy.

That brings me to the question I want to ask you, and it's a question you can only answer for yourself. The question is this: Has your formation in the Christian faith taught you how to enjoy and what to enjoy? Or has it simply taught you how and what to *use* in a more sophisticated way? When you look back on your life in thirty, forty, or fifty years' time, will you be able to say, "I enjoyed God, and helped others to do so, and I am ready to enjoy and be enjoyed by God forever"? Then, and perhaps only then, will you be able to say you've been a Christian. Because God's call to each one of us is, in the end, about just one word. *Enjoy.*